Will You Marry Me?

CHIFFONE NICOLE

Copyright 2009 by Chiffone Nicole Publishing

Will You Marry Me?
By Chiffone Nicole

ISBN: 978-0-615-34067-8

All rights reserved. No part of this book may be reproduced, stored in a retrieval system, or transmitted in any form or by any means – electronic, mechanical, photocopy, recording, or any other –except for brief quotations in printed reviews, without the prior written consent of the publisher. Unless otherwise indicated, all Scripture quotations are from the Amplified Version of the Bible.

Special quantity discounts may be available for bulk purchases for sales promotion, premiums, fundraising, educational or institutional use. For questions and comments, you may email the author and publisher at www.chiffonenicole.com for more information.

Printed in the United States of America

Book Editor by Idrissa N. Snider
www.idrissansnider.com

Front and Back Cover Design by Gwendolyn Jordan
www.bricays.com

Back cover photo by Kever Conyers

DEDICATION

This book is dedicated to the great women of integrity who hold on to the promises of God. In spite of what you have seen and experienced, you all still have hope that all things are possible with Christ.

AUTHOR'S NOTE

This work is nonfiction. The events and experiences detailed herein are all true and been retold to the best of my ability. Some names and identities have been changed in order to protect the integrity and representation of individuals involved. It is their right to tell their stories as they choose.

In regards to the Love Letters, they were given to me from spiritual utterance in which the Father spoke out His words. These letters are the messages that He wanted to impart into His daughters. I hope you enjoy them and get an understanding as I did.

                    In HIM,
                    Chiffone Nicole

ACKNOWLEDGMENTS

I would like to thank God for His grace and mercy. I cannot thank HIM enough; for all that He has done for me and been to me. Overall, I would like to thank God for Jesus my Savior. I especially want to thank Jesus for dying for me and living this life before I ever existed. Jesus went through it all and that ensures me that if I follow after Him that I can make it through any storm. I thank Jesus for leaving me a great comforter, the Holy Spirit. The Holy Spirit is a true way that I can communicate directly to the Father on a daily bases and it has truly changed my life.

I would like to thank my mother, Darlene N. Shelton for bringing me into to this world and giving me a foundation to seek the Father for myself. A special thanks to my spiritual mentors Gladys Guy and Verna Frye. I must acknowledge John Cooper, Elizabeth Copening, and Janice Gray for being well balanced. To my dear sister Valerie Tawwab, I thank you for your continued encouragement. I know our Dad has great joy about our beautiful sisterhood that has blossomed over the last three years. I also want to thank my friends that stood the test of time and prayed for me when I could not even pray for myself, Denene Byrd K. Watkins, T. Lewis and D. Williams. I especially want to thank two special friends that pushed and encouraged me towards completion of my assignment, Kamekio Lewis and Rashida Ivy.

To my dear son, JohnDavid thank you for loving me through the rough times. Your love for life has inspired me to walk in my destiny and live life with great joy. I know that as I walk in my destiny, I am training you to walk in yours. You have a special calling on your life, so reach for the stars and all your dreams will come true.

To my niece, Shanell Shelton, thank you for all the love and joy you have brought me over the years. I tried to be someone you could look up to. It's my prayer that you accomplish every desire that is in your heart. You have been a major part of my motivation to move forward in spite of the trials and tribulations.

I would like to thank my New Growth In Christ Church family especially the Prayer Ministry for my spiritual growth. I thank Apostle Sidney P. Malone, Pastor Brandon B. Porter, Prophet T. Hall, Pastor Lawrence J. London and the Late Pastor Guy; all of these wise men of God have influenced me and helped me get to this point in my life. I have a true honor and reverence for all of you, your positions and your dynamic Holy Spiritual teachings, Thank you!!!

God told me that He was going to edit my book and He sent me a dynamic and yielded vessel, Idrissa Snider who has much talent and capabilities. Idrissa Snider, I thank you for being my Aaron. You worked hard on my assignment and gave your prayers, input, and much wisdom and for that I am truly grateful. You took my words and thoughts and made it to be the art that God intended it to be. I know your finishing touches were orchestrated by God. Once again, I praise God for our Holy Spirit connection.

To Gwen Jordan, my graphic designer, I cannot thank you enough for your creativity. When God, gave me the vision on how the cover should look, little did I know that you would grasp the vision instantly. I know that without your obedience and you being in tune with the Spirit the cover would have not been what Daddy said it to be. I thank you for be being my third spiritual eye. You have been there since the beginning of *Will You Marry Me?* And your gift assisted with this production. I look forward to doing more Kingdom work with you.

Lastly, but certainly not least I would like to thank all my sisters in Christ who shared their stories that inspired me to complete my assignment from our Heavenly Father.

In HIM,
Chiffone Nicole.

†PRAYER†

Lord, I would like to thank you for this opportunity to present this invitation to your daughters. Heavenly Father let them know that you have heard their hurts, cries, and their deepest desires. Let them know that you are always with them in their time of struggle. Let them know that you love them at all times regardless of their flaws and sins. Daddy let their primary focus be on you and not on man. Lord restore hope, heal where there is pain, and replace sorrow with your unspeakable joy. Let your daughters know that in your time no good thing will be withheld. Be their guide, their friend, and their confidant. Lord let them walk so close with you that they are not anxious for anything, but they trust you to provide for them in all areas of their lives.

FOREWORD

As women, we are in search of love, not just any type of love but an intimate relationship with our soul mate. We seek someone to complete our sentences and for that matter, someone who will complete us. We search high and low for that special person to share out dearest secrets and our dreams to. We speak confidently on what we want in a mate and hopefully what he will bring to the table. We devote our time into learning his ways, his likes, and attempt to understand his flaws.

OH! My spirit is so moved by this because I searched for 16 years to find endearing love and I craved it in my heart and my soul. I did not even realize how bad and damaged I was. Having gone through many attacks of the enemy at an early stage in life, my heart and my soul were both in need of a healing. Healing needed to occur in order for the Holy Spirit to take me to where I had to go.

My head is so much clearer and I understand now. God has always spoken to me but I did not realize how true He was to His Word. Last Year He told me that I would be victorious and at that time my marriage to my husband of two years was twirling down and coming to an end. I was watching it slip away everyday: my job was not paying well and my house was facing foreclosure but God said to me, "Victorious" was He sure? I truly did not know God and did not let Him in. Ladies I have tears in my eyes because when I look back and share my story I cannot believe how my faith was shaken by a storm. Even though I knew the storm maker and regulator, I had major doubt. Well it is amazing, this thing we call life.

I was not only led to share my story but led to invite you on a date with Jesus. Come and meet a man that will cherish you, love you, and build you up with His purpose. A man, that if you only become His wife first; then your perfect mate will come to you. Ladies, princesses, God is asking you to come with Him on this date that will be unforgettable. Oh, how I love Him. He is everything that I looked for in a physical man. I needed to first meet the man who designed man, the original; the Alpha and Omega.

TABLE OF CONTENTS

Chapter 1	Unbroken Silence	1
Chapter 2	Learning Him	23
Chapter 3	Falling for Him	33
Chapter 4	Following His Purpose	41
Chapter 5	Understanding His Design	49
Chapter 6	Revelation	55
Chapter 7	Hope to My Sisters	63
Chapter 8	Remaining Focused	73
Chapter 9	Let Him Be Your Guide	81
Chapter 10	Trusting Him	87
Chapter 11	Him Trusting You	93
Chapter 12	Purpose: "Freeing Your Mind"	99
Chapter 13	Blessings: Honoring God	107
HIS PROMISE		115
THE ANSWER		119

CHAPTER 1

Unbroken Silence

One of my sisters in Christ advised me to look up the meaning of unbroken. After finding the meaning, a spiritual revelation came to me and once again I was amazed. The synonyms for the word unbroken are continuous, constant, steady, uninterrupted, complete and endless. When I look at all these words and think on my experiences I see one common factor, not being broken. When the word "silence" is added immediately the connotation changes. Historically women do not speak on brokenness in their marriages because of shame, fear, and what image they will portray. However, there is a shift taking place because it is time for healing and deliverance to happen in our lives.

When you declare, you make things possible. By releasing your faith it is soon to manifest in the natural. When Satan can get you to be silent, you then become powerless. When you repent you make it possible for God to forgive you and bless you. Let us all be honest, no one has always gotten life right and made all the right choices. However, some choices, especially those of sin, have deeper and longer consequences than those that are not.

I definitely can be honest and say that a lot of the pain I went through was self inflicted but as David states in Psalms 119, "It was good that I was afflicted that I might learn your statues." It also states that, "God's law being my delight; I would have perished in my affliction." The experience that I will share with you is a painful one. I felt a great deal of hurt and agony during this season. There are penalties when you ignore God's law and when you seek someone else more than you seek HIM. Also, remember that your words have power and lack of them is giving the power to Satan.

My Inspiration

When the Lord instructed me to write this book, I was not at all excited. The first feeling that I felt was shame because I knew that I had made a mess of my life. How was I going to share my story and to who? I also felt like I was the only one who had experienced gone through such pain. My other feeling was that of disbelief. I could not believe that I had failed so greatly. At that time, I had no idea that this experience would allow me to bless others. I am so glad that Daddy knew what He had for me.

I had gone back to the church, where I had attended the dynamic and life changing revival, to buy DVD's. I asked the sales associates who DVDs should I purchase and our conversation shifted to God's purpose. I began to share my story and they shared theirs. They told me how I had blessed them and they wanted to sow an offering into my life because I had encouraged them. As an offering, they gave me all the DVDs for free except for the one I had already paid for. I was afraid that people would think I was a fool for exposing myself but no, here were two women who were excited and blessed me.

The Prophet at the revival had told us that we were going to have visions, dreams and ideas. Though God had instructed me to write this book, I tried to pass on my idea to my spiritual mother but she did not accept. However, the silence had to be broken and the assignment had to be done, because there are women all around the world that need a healing and God has the cure.

God loves all my sisters in Christ, no matter our race or nationality. I recall shopping and a sales clerk from Germany shared her story. I always had strangers open up to me but this was different. For she told me intimate details about her marriage and how it had changed since she moved to America. She told me how she left her country to be with her husband and how her family had disowned her because she had married a black man. She went on to say that she was a single mother of a four year old son when they met, and shortly after they had a daughter together. She added that although they physically lived in the same home in which they saw one another on a day to day basis they did not even speak to each other, for several years. They were legally married, but they were spiritually estranged.

My response was disbelief, I thought wow, I moved miles away from my family but she had left her home country. She recalled having surgery and he told the doctor to have her call when she was done. Though the doctor had recommended him to stay he replied "No." She shared more details and I asked her about her relationship with the Father. She told me that she attended church and that she kept her marriage vows and did not cheat on her husband and worked three jobs to stay busy. She shared that her husband wanted her to leave but she refused.

I left that day and prayed for her in my car. I remember God told me that night that He wanted all His daughters to be healed and delivered. I knew that this book must be done. I knew God had something greater for His daughters......I knew that it was time to break the silence...

The Lord had given me I Peter 5:7 where it discussed identical sufferings. Little did I know for a whole year that women would share their experiences with me. Little did I know that it was time to share my story. Finally, I was convinced and inspired to tell my story to help women all over the world.

Although I had some knowledge of marriage, when I look back I realize I actually had none. It is like saying you understand something but when you are given the test, you have no idea what you are doing. You say to yourself, I did not learn this. Why is this on the test? This can't be the information I learned. All the time you are still failing. Or perhaps you have taken the wrong class and the credit hours do not count toward your major. Therefore you have delayed your graduation. Even Though you have wasted time, you might have still learned something. Well, this was my approach towards deciding to marry.

Unfortunately, I always have thought like a social worker, meaning I could accept and help anybody. I used my social worker beliefs to justify why I was making a choice that would hurt me so badly. Ladies I was a hurt person prior to my marriage but to get hurt again I was like "Ok life is really not fair." Having a bad childhood, I was sure that my adulthood would be so much brighter. Therefore, I figured that I would have a good marriage. So if you assumed that I expected pity from one teacher because I had failed with another, you are probably right. However, we all know that teachers are not going to give you an "A" for pity.

When you say "yes" to something you are supposed to be purposed for it and prepared for it. We cannot get away from the Word of God, 2 Corinthians 6:14 clearly states to not be unequally yoked and it tells us that lightness and darkness have nothing in common. God gives us instruction on how to make Godly choices and wise choices. He tells us. Ladies we must not ignore God's Word, He warns us and we must listen. God is our father and He knows what is best for us. He also knows what He wants for us, but we must slow down, be patient and listen to Him. We must have a conversation with Him and not ourselves. A conversation is not one sided, we must give God an opportunity to speak back to us and be willing to accept what He says and trust Him. Deceit is real and we can be our own worst enemy when we do not seek HIM First.

Since I was 16 years old I wanted someone to fill that void in my life – A void that stemmed from an abusive childhood. Because of this deep set emptiness I craved for affection badly. I believed that I would receive this love from a relationship with a man. I was a woman who went from one pretend relationship to the next. I say "pretend" because I was never anyone's girlfriend but always the second best or one of many. I had no self respect and low self esteem; both allowed me to play the game for over ten years. It is funny how I wanted so desperately for some man to love me but I did not even love myself. I did not even know whose I was or who I was. Though I was successful with college degrees and loved God and was in church for most of my life, I was not living how God wanted me to. I was doing what I wanted the majority of the time and God's will some of the time. The Word refers to that way of living as lukewarm and the world refers to it as human. Unfortunately, when you disobey your parents there are consequences and you're going have to go through them.

My Real Story

I had been going from relationship to relationship and out of the blue I received a phone message from Immanuel. I questioned how he got my home number and I ignored his call. Shortly after, when I was with a mutual friend, he called her and asked to speak to me. It was a major surprise because we had not spoken in over eight years. Besides, this was a guy who I had a crush on, my best friend's older brother. That being the case, I did not expect him to actually have genuine feelings for me. I also could not imagine sleeping with him because that was my friend's brother. So, that line had never been crossed, he was simply an innocent crush.

I remember when I first saw Immanuel, ladies he was charming. He was walking into his mother's house as I waited for his sister to come out. I thought he is "so cute", even though he had a slight limp. All I saw that day was the sparkle in his eyes. I was gone at that moment. Although the Word says he that finds a wife, finds a good thing and finds favor. I know that I spotted him first because at the time I was very aggressive. Once we were engaged, he shared with me that his first thought of me was, "look at this fast girl looking at me."

He later confessed to his mother that he would one day marry me, I still sought him first. In the past his mother told me that I was looking for love in all the wrong places. I heard her, but I could not change my desire and honestly I did not see a need to. I needed that void filled.

Immanuel went down his path and I went down mine. Then eight years later we spoke again. When I talked to him I blushed and he stated that I had made his heart smile. I was like "wow" and did not even know that comment was words from a song. I believed him to be sincere. We talked that night for hours. He expressed that he came back into my life to get his wife back. I was blown away and in two days he asked me to marry him via phone and I actually said, "Yes." Even though, I had not seen this man in over eight years, and he lived 12 hours away. Most importantly, I did not seek God on my decision but I acted out of my emotions. For weeks to come I looked forward to it and became more excited about confirmations from others but I did not seek God for his true approval. Now I know that true confirmation lines up with the Word of God. However, back then I had already made a commitment and it was becoming real each day.

Immanuel shared with me that finances would be our biggest concern because he was not making enough money to support us solely. Although he was straight forward with me, I believed that we would make it. I even over looked the fact that I would probably be laid off soon. My rational was to move quickly to support Immanuel with this new business venture.

Less than two weeks later Immanuel came to see me. We had not seen each other in over eight years so we were extremely excited. That is when I actually learned a little about him. For instance he had a clothing store with his brother. We talked about having a new business and starting a restaurant together. I also learned that he had a daughter and did not want any more children because the world was a bad place and I felt the same at the time. We had so much in common. He and I both considered living on a private island.

At that stage in my life I truly believed that I had found my soul mate. What convinced me that he loved me was when I shared with him my biggest fear, which was that I had never had an HIV test and vowed that I would only get one if I was ever to become pregnant. He immediately responded that we would go to Thailand to get the cure. Immanuel made me feel like he would accept me no matter what. I believed him and became vulnerable. Based on his response to my fear, I was convinced that he was the one.

I told him about my relationship with God and how church was a big part of my life. His response was that he was willing to go to church with me twice a month. This should have been a red flag because I was in church two to three times a week, but I accepted this. I explained to him that I needed to check with my pastor about us because I valued his input. Immanuel was extremely upset because he felt that he had to wait for the approval from another man. In the past he claimed to be a Muslim but denied it with me.

He seemed well versed on religion but I was somewhat alarmed. None the less I still proceeded forward. When Immanuel came to town he asked me again to marry him and I said yes, again. We went around to our family and announced our engagement.

That year I made a couple of road trips in order to see where I would be living. Yes, I was leaving my family, my home, and my idea job.

On our wedding day it stormed like no other time before. When I came out, the rain suddenly stopped and immediately following our wedding vows the sun came out. It was very hot but the skies were clear and the weather was beautiful. I was convinced that this was a message from God, and He was letting me know that there would be storms but the sun would come out. At the spiritual level I was on, I truly believed that our marriage would be brighter. I had no clue.

Even though the storms came I was not in a place as a wife to handle them. I cried more than I prayed. I worried and had anxiety day in and day out. Yes I went to church and Immanuel did too. We were so happy at first, but it only takes a second to take your eyes off the road to cause an accident. I was not the wife that I needed to be. Our marriage was built on sand, not a solid foundation. I had no idea of what I had done, not the devil, but what I had done…

After we were married I stayed in Detroit and attempted to move south. However, my grandmother was diagnosed with cancer and there was no way I could leave her that way. Immanuel understood and he went back without me. I waited until my grandmother was discharged from the hospital. It meant a lot to me because my grandmother was the only person who was happy for me. My family was so upset that I was moving so far away and I had very limited "well wishes" offered.

When I moved, I became homesick and worried about our finances. We were waiting for a small business loan. This loan would help us with the restaurant. Meanwhile, we both took jobs to make ends meet. We stayed in his family house and that drove me absolutely crazy. I was happy that Immanuel came home to me every night, but I had to share him with other family members on a daily basis. We were somewhat happy in the beginning. We laughed and talked and went to the movies often. I desired to have a son but he felt that it was not time, I agreed, not knowing I was pregnant at the time. We began to have little disagreements and they developed into something more.

My husband felt so much pressure because my house in Detroit had not sold. We had major debt. Our money was limited, but he had a plan and I still believed we would be ok. His focus was our finances and mine were on my feelings.

My old job was still available and I was frustrated because I could not find employment that was paying what I was accustomed to. So naturally I went back to my job that had status and perks.

I did one of the worst things you could do; I separated myself from my husband. To rectify the situation I kept implying that I could fix our finances. I also implied that I was the rescuer and the breadwinner. Even though our business loan went through, I left after only two months of being with him. This action opened so many doors. We began to argue more and I said the one phrase you do not ever say, "I want a divorce."

When I spoke divorce, Satan heard me. At the time I felt good about asking for a divorce, I was back in my home state with the people who loved me and I had a job that paid well. I felt that I did not need him and I had no idea that I was carrying our son. I found out the same day that I was pregnant but I had already disrespected my husband. I had invited the devil in my marriage. In my heart I knew that my marriage changed that day. As wives, we give life to marriages; life can only come from a woman. When we stop carrying out our portion destruction comes in. I warn you my sisters in Christ, watch the words you say and reverence your husband it is so…..important. You may think that is just the way you are, but that allows so many other problems to come in when you disrespect him.

Well Immanuel took me up North and he went back to the South. One of my many consequences of separating from my husband was my ideal job did a hiring freeze. Yes a hiring freeze, after they had me leave my new life. I was pregnant with no insurance, no job and my husband lived 12 hours away. Even though I was dead wrong, God still blessed me with health care and a part time job. The hiring freeze lasted for about six weeks and then I returned to my career. I could not see the truth and did not consider my family.

After the move, Immanuel viewed me differently and felt that I did not believe in him anymore. He became distant with me and when we did communicate he spoke coldly towards me. His words were harsh and his underling insults devastated me. Along with the verbal abuse he did not desire to be intimate with me anymore. During this time I still had no idea what I had done to his masculinity and that increased my pain.

Besides the fact that Immanuel did some painful things to me later, I can honestly admit that I ruined our marriage in more ways than one. I was not well equipped or knowledgeable about the role of a wife. I could not leave my past behind and allow myself to pray that God would let him be the provider that He called all men to be. I got in the way and I did not make the appropriate adjustments. I still had that independent attitude and went into a marriage with a carnal way of thinking. I did not truly seek God. I only checked with myself. Submission was not my strong point but my emotions were. You cannot allow your emotions to rule you. You cannot bring the old in with the new, when you are trying to move forward.

Meanwhile, my pregnancy was not an easy one. The doctor believed my son to be dead. I had severe bleeding, so I was on bed rest for several weeks which was difficult because Immanuel was not able to stay up North with me. He was trying to start our business so I could return before the baby was born. After I made the move back North, our conversations changed. He did not even want to talk to me because I reminded him of more responsibilities. I was about to give birth soon and some of the business loans were being used to pay bills. We took out more loans, more credit cards, and our debts accumulated rapidly.

After having our healthy baby boy, JohnDavid, I moved two weeks later to be with Immanuel. In the midst of all our problems, I still believed that if we would be fine. However, I knew in my heart, that he did not want me. I figured that if I could prove to him how much I loved him and that I had been wrong to put the job before him, I could gain his affection again.

When I went back, Immanuel's relationship with his brother was closer than our union. They started their second clothing store together, and they were buying houses next door to each other and he did not inform me first. I became so angry because of all the secrets and that he had replaced me with his brother. He seemed to have no desire to tell me our marriage was over. I thought this cannot be; besides we are married and I just had his son. Why would he not talk to me? Why was everything between him and his brother? Then that day happened I called him out his name and it sealed it for him.

JohnDavid was six weeks old, and we found out that he had to have surgery because of a hernia. During the doctor's visit, I pleaded with him to work on our marriage. He told me that he was not certain because I did not respect him anymore. I went from one storm to another storm in my life. I felt that my world was collapsing and I received more horrible news from up North.

The aunt who raised me was diagnosed with cancer and I returned to my home state to see about her. Immanuel bought me a plane ticket to visit for seven days. He did not accompany me but went to California for our business. While I was there he called me and asked me did I even want to come back to him, and did I want to stay up north. I knew in that conversation this was his way of telling me it was over but I replied, "I want to come back to you." Even with a brand new home and the fact that I had resigned from my job, our marriage was still over.

I could not believe that our marriage was over and our sex life did not exist. He gave numerous reasons why he would not have sex with me. I became depressed and felt completely unattractive. No matter my attempts and advances he would not touch me. I began to question my performance and his faithfulness. Two of the major reasons he gave for not being intimate with me was that he did not want me pregnant again and the other reason was that he was only focused on our finances. I still could not bear the pain of lying next to my husband and him not touching me. I recall a time when I set the mood with candle light and wore special lingerie. Immanuel came in our bedroom and kissed our son who was asleep and attempted to play with him. He made it obvious in that moment that no matter what I tried, he was not interested. It is amazing how I watched sex be used as a weapon towards me. When I was single, I committed fornication for years and when I was married I was denied. Ladies, if you allow Satan to play on your fears and emotions, he **will** have a ball!

Due to my frustrations in my marriage, I requested counseling from church and we went. During counseling, he cried tears because he said that when I left him he could not forgive me. I did not believe that he was serious. I knew I had hurt him but I did not think I had done something unforgivable; besides I did not commit adultery. I tried to make it right by resigning from my job in front of him with a smile. I tried to reassure him that I was committed to our family but he would not let it go. I began to feel rejected and extremely frustrated. I recalled when I refused to forgive and held grudges. I would not free others and now the same thing was happening to me. I thought this is different. I had given up everything and had his son but he was still saying, "I don't forgive you."

A couple of months later my aunt passed away and my husband did not accompany me for support to the funeral. He did not even call me on the day of her burial and did not even answer his phone. I knew that it was over but I still tried to pray and fix our marriage. I went back to my beautiful five bedroom house. A home with no love in it....

For months Immanuel claimed to be working late to save our house. However, late hours became days. He would come home with no apology or explanations. He would take a shower and change clothes and leave again. On Friday nights he would get dressed up, and I knew he was taking someone out. At times I would call making threats to come and find him. Sometimes it worked but most of time he cared less. One day, I checked his phone that had a text message from another woman. The text shared that she had missed him. I spoke to her and she said that she sent the text accidentally to him instead of her husband. To this day Immanuel shares that he may have done many wrong things in our union but never had he been unfaithful. Though I did not believe him, I am ok with it because it is the past.

We argued more and more. A couple months later we had a big blow up and he took his ring off and said that he was done. Though I had taken mine off several times, he had never taken off his. I called my mother in law and he had already told her that we were over. What had I done? I had done it again, reacted in my soul and not in my spirit. I allowed my emotions to rule me and did not seek God for guidance and an answer.

That late spring I sought to get closer to God. I received the precious gift to speak in the spirit. I begin to attend prayer twice a week. I finally took my focus off of Immanuel. I begin to learn how to feed my spirit. By that time so much had been done in the marriage. We were losing our business and our home. Immanuel solely focused on saving our home, and I focused on my faith.

I returned to work. I still had hope and believed that as long as we had each other that we would bounce back. That was not the case. Immanuel became more irritable and pulled further away. During this season I did not use profanity towards him. God had delivered me and I had some peace. I meditated on His Word day and night, but Immanuel became unbearable the closer I got to Christ. The Lord led me to the book of Titus which prepared me for the lost of my home. I tried to comfort Immanuel as well about losing our home, but he stopped attending church services and his faith appeared to decrease.

Though we went two months without arguing, we still separated. I tried to reverence Immanuel because I believed what the Word said. I recalled the day of our separation. I was at church and he was trying to reach me. My phone was on silent. I had stayed for both services because I worked in children's church and attended the second service. Immanuel had called around looking for me. He had asked me to pick up something from another church member. After service, I checked my voice mail and I had a message from him. On the message, this man was completely going off on me. I was so confused and hurt by his anger. I called my friend and he had called her downing me and using profanity about me to her. I had enough and I snapped. When I went home and

Unbroken Silence

encountered him, I did not use profanity but I went at him. I threw a bottle of seasoning on the counter and told him he would not disrespect me anymore. I then told him, he could leave. He left a week before our 2nd anniversary. Immanuel was gone. I could not believe it. I spent our anniversary with one of my sister's in Christ and my son. We were separated.

With us being separated, I could not believe I had to face foreclosure by myself. However, in the midst of this large storm, God became HIM; He filled the void of my husband and stepped in when I needed Him the most. Even with two foreclosures on my credit, unpaid loans and credit cards, I was approved for an apartment. I knew that God was right there.

I was not sure how I was going to pay my rent because I did not make much. But God had told me months before that I would be victorious. Little did I know the Prayer Ministry had helped and changed my life for the better. I begin receiving blessings and favor. I had the best husband in God. I did not even realize how special I was to Him. He was showing me that He was my sole provider.

Determined to do better and provide for my son, I went on many interviews and I had many offers. Unfortunately, the pay was the same. I believed God for something better. I recall speaking to a dear friend and sharing with her that my brakes needed to be replaced and that I needed car insurance. I talked to her and she blessed me with one thousand dollars. God spoke a few words to me on that day; I AM God. I was amazed. I was able to get things done.

Not even a week later the Lord told me to write my son's name on my offering of five dollars. Though I questioned God, I was obedient. I still paid my tithes because I believed God although in the natural I could not afford it, but in the spirit I could not afford not to. I had no idea that we were having an appreciation day and giveaways. I won the grand prize. It was five hundred dollars paid out to my apartment. I could not believe how good God was taking care of my son and me. That same month, I got the job that put me back to the salary that I was accustomed to. Now I could afford to take care of my son.

In this season I still wanted my Immanuel back. Although, I had God, I still wanted him. During this time he still had no desire to come back to me. I remember him looking me eye to eye and telling me that I was not his wife and that he did not love me anymore. During this time he did not come around often. It hurt to know that, he was missing time with his son. But I had to give JohnDavid the same gift that had been given to me, Jesus. In this season he had a Heavenly Father who had been there and would be there always.

It is weird how I look back over this situation and I am certain that all things worked for my good. Even though it did not feel good when Immanuel was not around, I kept my focus on the Father and allowed Him to work on me. I remember that in this season, I learned how to truly walk in love with Immanuel. Though I had not been able to pray for Immanuel constantly while we were together, I did so when we were a part. My motives and desires both changed to pleasing the Father.

I recall when I prayed for Immanuel. My chest was hurting and I could barely breathe. I had taken on his pain. Finally, I could understand the hurt he had been feeling. Now when I prayed, it was not for us to get back together but for him to reunite with the Father, so he would be healed. So I kept praying for him more, although I wish I would have done so when we were together.

While the Lord continued to work on me, I became more compassionate for Immanuel. I could not ask God for another husband if I did not make this right with the first one. Though Immanuel hurt me, I had done the same to him. We both had been used by the devil. I know we would like to blame someone when we experience something horrible but the Word says that we wrestle against spirits and not people.

As time went by God had made me whole. My confidence in HIM came and my self confidence improved greatly. I was finally able to stay focused and God healed me from my past. I was finally able to ask Immanuel for my key back to my apartment. Even though he only had the key for convenience to see our son at times. I needed to take it back and establish boundaries between us. Once I asked for the key, he knew I was serious about moving forward. Though I knew we soon would be divorced, our relationship in the spiritual sense was healed. Immanuel was excited about what God had done in my life, and I was excited what God had done for him.

The power of forgiveness is great and rewarding. Forgiveness allows you to release and receive what God has for you. A part of the healing process is to forgive others in order to release the hurt and pain for you. God wants to heal us but we must forgive in order for it to occur. Ladies, God has the power to make you whole but only if you let him.

The closer I became to God and allowed myself to grow, Immanuel's life started to improve for the better. In my heart I wanted God's best for him and for him to experience the Father on the same level. How could I truly say that I loved Christ but not walk in love with one of His sons. God loves him, the real Immanuel. The evil spirits entered in both of us during our marriage. God saw past our imperfections, our sins, and flawed characteristics. He accepts us for who we are and then He purges us and develops us to what He called us to be. We must not hold others to their past offenses. Instead we should pray that they will come in the full knowledge of Christ. We must see others the way God see them. God was so patient with me during my process. Therefore, I know I must be patient with others, while they are growing.

PRAYER
Unbroken Silence

    Lord my prayer for my sisters is that you fill their hearts with so much of your love that it empowers them to forgive themselves and others. Lord let them know when they repent of their sins that they can move forward with you. Let them know that though they have been through a storm that you are the inner peace that they need. Lord let them look to you for real love and true love.
    AMEN, so be it.

FORGIVENESS
Scriptures

And whenever you stand praying, if you have anything against anyone, forgive him and let it drop (leave it, let it go), in order that your Father Who is in heaven may also forgive you your [own] failings and shortcomings and let them drop. But if you do not forgive, neither will your Father in heaven forgive your failings and shortcomings. Mark 11:25-26

For if you forgive people their trespasses [their reckless and willful sins, leaving them, letting them go, and giving up resentment], your heavenly Father will also forgive you. Matthew 6:14

Then Peter came up to Him and said, Lord, how many times may my brother sin against me and I forgive him and let it go? [As many as] up to seven times? Matthew 18:21

And forgive us our sins, for we ourselves also forgive everyone who is indebted to us [who has offended us or done us wrong]. And bring us not into temptation but rescue us from evil. Luke 11:4

And even if he sins against you seven times in a day, and turns to you seven times and says, I repent [I am sorry], you must forgive him (give up resentment and consider the offense as recalled and annulled). Luke 17:4

[Now having received the Holy Spirit, and being led and directed by Him] if you forgive the sins of anyone, they are forgiven; if you retain the sins of anyone, they are retained. John 20:23

Be gentle and forbearing with one another and, if one has a difference (a grievance or complaint) against another, readily pardoning each other; even as the Lord has [freely] forgiven you, so must you also [forgive]. Colossians 3:13

Unbroken Silence

HEALING FOR THE SOUL
Scriptures

Confess to one another therefore your faults (your slips, your false steps, your offenses, your sins) and pray [also] for one another, that you may be healed and restored [to a spiritual tone of mind and heart]. The earnest (heartfelt, continued) prayer of a righteous man makes tremendous power available [dynamic in its working]. James 5:16

You have made known to me the ways of life; You will enrapture me [diffusing my soul with joy] with and in Your presence. Acts 2:28

Establishing and strengthening the souls and the hearts of the disciples, urging and warning and encouraging them to stand firm in the faith, and [telling them] that it is through many hardships and tribulations we must enter the kingdom of God. Acts 14:22

And now [brethren], I commit you to God [I deposit you in His charge, entrusting you to His protection and care]. And I commend you to the Word of His grace [to the commands and counsels and promises of His unmerited favor]. It is able to build you up and to give you [your rightful] inheritance among all God's set-apart ones (those consecrated, purified, and transformed of soul). Acts 20-32

So get rid of all uncleanness and the rampant outgrowth of wickedness, and in a humble (gentle, modest) spirit receive and welcome the Word which implanted and rooted [in your hearts] contains the power to save your souls. James 1:21

When my soul fainted upon me [crushing me], I earnestly and seriously remembered the Lord; and my prayer came to You, into Your holy temple. Jonah 2:7

CHAPTER 2

Learning Him

In order to learn our beautiful and magnificent Father you must spend time with Him. You must meditate, read, and study His Word. You must learn what He values and what is important to Him. You must learn how to please HIM. You must learn His ways. You must learn what He hates and what He loves. You must learn the character of God. You must review His résumé.

Who do others say God is? What makes Him a great Lord? It takes time to learn HIM but when you do, you fall for HIM. How can you not? During the healing and growth process of the divorce, I fasted throughout the year on my own and with my church family. During this time He revealed so much to me through His Word and the Holy Spirit. The scriptures I read became clearer.

I desired to learn more of His Word and I decided to attend my church ministry training class. I had no intention of being in ministry but I only desired to learn more of God's Word. The class added to my knowledge and my spiritual growth. It explained to me the things that I had been experiencing but had no titles and true meanings of them. I learned a great deal about whom God was and His capabilities.

I have been so amazed on learning who God truly is and who He has been in my life. Having a hurtful childhood, I was fortunate to learn about Him early in life. He has been a mother, a father, and my husband during many trials and tribulations. Over the years I have had different levels of intimacy but during my relationship with Immanuel I learned how God intends for us to be close with others. I remember when I went through in my marriage, and became intimate with Christ. He continually showed himself to me as a provider, Jehovah Jireh. He kept on taking care of me with many dynamic blessings. I mean I watched Him be my husband over and over again. I truly thank Him for His unconditional love that has no end. God's pure love rained on me.

I remember I was in need of a car. Daddy knew what I needed and His word says that He will supply all our needs. I searched high and low for a used twenty year old Lexus but my credit would not allow me a good interest rate. The Lord had told me for several weeks that He had made provisions. Little did I know that He had a brand new Luxury car waiting for me. I thought, could, "I be approved for a brand new car?" My credit score was in the mid four hundreds. However, the financial manager heard my story and had compassion, and I pulled out the parking lot. We as Christians know that favor and faith works better than your credit score.

After having no money for daycare expenses from purchasing the car, I went to church and was blessed. I walked in service and they were giving the children workers one hundred dollars for providing service to the church. I was so amazed because it was the amount I needed for JohnDavid's childcare expenses. I was so grateful how God kept blessing me that weekend; I cannot even explain fully what I felt at that time.

Though I had this beautiful car, the payment was high but the Lord had already stated that He had made provision. He had done so, I just needed to trust Him and it would work out. I must admit I was confused and stressed out because they sent me a letter that stated I was not approved. When I called they informed me that I needed more money or a co signer. I was upset because I had the car for almost three weeks and felt that this was my vehicle. After asking for help from others, it was finally put on my heart to ask my mother. She did so and had the exact amount for the additional payment. My payments went down almost half of the original loan. God spoke to me later and stated that He did not do it for me but for Him to receive the glory.

When I say God continued blessing me, He did. I remember wanting a layaway out but not having the funds and really needing the shoes. It was the last day for me to get the layaway. I was looking for the receipt and found money in an envelope to cover the cost of the shoes. God spoke to me so clearly, "Go get your shoes." It was weird because it felt like "my husband" was sending me to shopping. I knew that He was my husband at that point, and it felt weird but good. But that's how God is. You can't explain His goodness. He is best provider that any woman could have.

On the same day I was invited for dinner and treated by a church member. Though I had money left over from the shoes, God still took me out and expenses were paid by Him. I mean God will be whatever you allow Him to be. However, God is a gentleman. He will not force Himself on you; He will only come in if He is invited.

After I allowed Him to be a provider and my husband, He became my deliverer. He delivered me from depression. This was an illness that I fought and struggled with since I was a teenager. Even though I was social worker, I never had treatment. I watched God change me and my soul was made whole. My emotions had stopped ruling and running my life and now I was being led by the Holy Spirit and the real me, my spirit. I finally matured in HIM, I got it. It has never been about me but about His Kingdom being done on earth.

During this process God also became my protector. I watched Him protect me from myself and others. There were two men that I became interested in, one from my past and another from my church. The one from my past, I talked to several times via phone but the last time I tried to reach him the calls kept dropping. I was still determined to speak to him and once we did, he told me in the conversation that he was seeing someone else.

In regards to the other gentlemen I observed him at a church event and he appeared very flirty with the other women and instantly my feelings for him changed. I refused to not use discernment when involving myself with a man again. The Word tells us to be watchful as well as prayerful.

So many times we ignore the obvious and proceed forward. All the time we are setting ourselves up for failure. Most of times by a week of conversation with someone, we hear and see things that do not match our values or should I say God's values but we ignore and pretend they do not exist. I did this for years because I thirsted for a soul mate. In the beginning I did not even complain, I just proceeded forward. The Word of God tells us to guard our hearts, Proverbs 4:2.

In both situations I knew God was protecting me from myself and my emotions. The teachings of my pastor, describes to us the three components of who we are: flesh, soul, and spirit. The flesh is our body and it tells us how we feel. Example of the body, you may not feel like going to work but you must go because you have responsibilities, so you ignore your feelings.

The soul is your will, desires, and emotions. I had a difficult time grasping this concept in more than one area. I wanted to do things my way and how could I know what was the best thing for me. I played church often, claiming that it

Learning Him

was God's will but my actions did not line up with God's purpose. As I have stated before in regard to my desires, my true desire was a man's love and not truly desiring the creator.

My emotions were all over the place majority of time. I did not even realize that my emotions ruled me. I knew I suffered from highs and lows but I did not know how to manage it. I seriously thought about medication as an out because at some points it was becoming more difficult for me to cope. Even though I was in church most of the week, I was weak and fragile. I recall being in prayer, and just moments later after going to the nursery to assist my baby I would be extremely emotionally distraught. My son would play and I was the one laid out in tears. Though I felt this bad, ladies, I kept seeking Him. I knew that God was who He said He was; I just had to experience Him for myself. I was determine to be healed and made whole.

Lastly you have your spirit, the real you. Your spirit is how God communicates with you. The spirit is the only one that should govern your life. I am so thankful that the day of my deliverance came. I was set free from all the anxieties, depression, mood swings, and the emotional roller coaster that I had been on. For once in my life I had so much joy and peace and it stayed with me. I remember the first time that I cried after I had been delivered; it was not over the top. Normally when I cried about one thing, I thought of everything bad in my life, I would become depressed. But now, when I cried it was for the particular situation and I was able to come out quickly and move forward in prayer. Yes our bodies and emotions are both normal but just like everything in life they have their place, but never first place. I pray that God will give you balance in your lives and bring your spirit man to the front, so you can walk in your destiny.

I thought I was ready to date, but it was not the time and my focus still needed to be on Him. I was over my husband but I was not legally divorced. I realized that it was important to walk in integrity during the process. Shortly after, God promised me in due season that He would give me a new husband. However, God is a God of order and in due season means, when it is time it would occur. Other men tried to approach me but I was waiting on greatness because HE is great. I honestly could not confuse that in that season, I continued to enjoy the time of being one on one with Him. I was learning Him and spending my time with only Him. No worries or distractions, but trying to love on Him, how He loves on me. I saw this period as a time for healing and preparing me for my next.

It is so important to not take old ways and thoughts into a new marriage. I want the way that I handle my new marriage, to be God's way. I know that God can direct you on how to interact with your mate, how to pray for him, and most important how to love him.

Love is an action word. Be led by the Holy Spirit and the Word God will show and teach you how to show God's love. Love is about giving of yourself and being selfless. The more you love on others; it will come back to you. If you are not praying for the man that you are with and loving him the way you should, who is? He needs to be lifted up to stay in his role as the head of the household. When we move away from the word, remember consequences come. Love is not only defined as action but Love is God and God is love.

A part of learning HIM, is knowing what He expects for you. How can I know what He has for me if I truly do not know HIM? I attended ministry class to learn more about HIM because I was intrigued by HIM. I found myself desiring His word, instruction, and His presence. The more I sought HIM, the more He revealed about Himself.

The ministry class was truly was dynamic. It required me to study the Word and research it. Oh what spiritual revelation I received. I was required to write papers and take

Learning Him

several exams. I was able to be around other believers who were filled with the spirit and believed God was awesome.

You learn HIM by studying HIM. That is the way you find out about who He is and who He says He is to you. I cannot describe it any better how amazing He is to me. He is so great; just seek HIM and you will see how real He is. It takes time to learn someone and it also takes desire to want to learn HIM. Why not learn the man who has the great plan for your life. I know that there is so much more to learn about HIM that I cannot even conceive. It is like falling in love with the same person over and over again. Just when you think that you know HIM, He shows a totally different side that you never knew existed.

Who is God? This question is short but, the answer is infinite with such long meaning. God is the beginning and end. God is strong, dependable, reliable, and perfection at its best. God is love and order. God is the definition of integrity and loyal to all His Word. Someone you can truly count on. He has come through and will come through again. A true friend or should I say best friend. God is dynamic, awesome, and great magnificent. These are just a few that describe who He is. God, the King of Kings is love. God is everything at its best. God is the Prince of Peace. God is a confidant.

PRAYER
Learning HIM

    Lord I pray that your daughters will seek you more in this season and that you reveal yourself to them. Lord I pray that they will learn your ways. Lord that my sisters learn and apply your kingdom principles. Lord I pray that they are always opened to seek you and your wisdom. Lord, give them the desire to thirst for your Word daily.
    AMEN, so be it.

Learning Him

WISDOM
Scriptures

The reverent fear and worship of the Lord is the beginning of Wisdom and skill [the preceding and the first essential, the prerequisite and the alphabet]; a good understanding, wisdom, and meaning have all those who do [the will of the Lord]. Their praise of Him endures forever. [Job. 28:28; Prov. 1:7; Matt. 22:37, 38; Rev. 14:7.] Psalm 111:10

For the Lord gives skillful and godly Wisdom; from His mouth come knowledge and understanding. Proverbs 2:6

God replied to Solomon, Because this was in your heart and you have not asked for riches, possessions, honor, and glory, or the life of your foes, or even for long life, but have asked wisdom and knowledge for yourself, that you may rule and judge My people over whom I have made you king, 2 Chronicles 1:11

He hides away sound and godly Wisdom and stores it for the righteous (those who are upright and in right standing with Him); He is a shield to those who walk uprightly and in integrity, Proverbs 2:7

Prize Wisdom highly and exalt her, and she will exalt and promote you; she will bring you to honor when you embrace her. Proverbs 4:8

For whoever finds me [Wisdom] finds life and draws forth and obtains favor from the Lord. Proverbs 8:35

He who gains Wisdom loves his own life; he who keeps understanding shall prosper and find good. Proverbs 19:8

And we are setting these truths forth in words not taught by human wisdom but taught by the [Holy] Spirit, combining and interpreting spiritual truths with spiritual language [to those who possess the Holy Spirit]. 1 Corinthians 2:13

[For I always pray to] the God of our Lord Jesus Christ, the Father of glory, that He may grant you a spirit of wisdom and revelation [of insight into mysteries and secrets] in the [deep and intimate] knowledge of Him, Ephesians 1:17

CHAPTER 3

Falling for Him

When I refer to our Heavenly Father as "Daddy" it is because I view that word as an affectionate term. I also refer to Him as my Husband because He will be whatever you need Him to be. But to take it further He will be what you allow Him to be. Lately, I have been seeing how He is a gentleman in which, the Lord He will not force himself on anyone. Those are qualities I expect to see in my new husband. Gentlemen qualities that I never paid close attention to or cared about, I now expect them in my new. Yes, I want to be that virtuous woman but I must know how to be treated like a lady, and act in the role of a virtuous woman that honors and pleases God.

During my process the Lord spoke several promises to me. He gave me instructions and answers that I would later come to understand. He told me to let Him work, to walk in love, and to speak to HIM. He instructed me to yield to Him and to let go. He kept encouraging and instructed me not to have anymore anxieties. He spoke to give Him His do praise because when praise goes up blessings come down. He told me to have faith, He told me to stay focused and not be distracted. God said that He loved me and that I did not even know how much. I know so because He told me that He had a perfect plan for my life. He asked me talk to Him and trust Him. He asked me to fall in love with Him, as well as His Word.

The Father explained in His Word was victory, peace, understanding, and wisdom. He told me to inherit the full knowledge of HIM, walk in understanding, walk in forgiveness, and to walk in a manner that demonstrates His way. The Lord asked, "What would I do in situations?" He told me to watch my words and thoughts. He told me, "When the enemy attacks, to fight with the Word of God." He reminded me that the evil one comes to kill and destroy. But that I would have protection because I was chosen. He said that the blood of Jesus covered me and angels guarded me. He told me to come closer to Him and be intimate with HIM and admonished me to study His ways and to stay in the gospel; the New Testament. Read what I have written, He explained, in doing so I discovered that His Word did not change. He repeated that He loved me and told me trust Him, not man. But the Lord emphasized to love man, but to first trust Him with all my heart. As the Holy Spirit continued to minister to me He told me to dream. He concluded that He is Holy, and instructed me to stay in fellowship with Him, my Father.

The Lord told me to write down what He instructed because He covered so many areas that night. This conversation was the beginning of many to come. He said that I was healed now and no more about Immanuel or my marriage. He stated for me to leave it alone and to walk in love. Stay focused on Him and His Kingdom principles and life, not the past. Know that the same applies to you. The Father is telling you that you are beautiful inside and out. He stated that He has a great work for you to do. He instructed me to take off my problems because they were there attempting to distract me. He rebuked the spirits of suicide and depression and sent it back to hell. He demanded the evil one to leave my home and commanded generational curses to be broken.

Falling for Him

He shared that generation's curses would not touch my son's life. Lastly, He repeated to me to yield to HIM.

Ladies, it is funny how we spend so much time with our new beau. We try to figure everything there is to know about him. We want to know his likes, dislikes and his way, everything. We are so curious about the new man. We want to spend so much time with him. We want to go out and have a blast! We want to be treated like his number one and only. We want him to like the way we wear our hair, clothes, and our style. We especially want him to understand the way we think and to know our thoughts.

The same desire should go towards knowing God in an intimate way by, seeking His attention and His perfect love. Fall head over heels for Him. Wake up with a smile and thinking on spending one on one time with Him. Learning His ways, His truths, daydreaming, and concentrating on Him all day and night. It is like wanting the DJ to play our favorite song; while we are at work, staring off because we are thinking about the goodness of God, allowing Him to hold us close and feeling His presence. When we become so focused on Him that we have peace in the midst of a great storm; bragging on His goodness, His latest accomplishments, and His success. Knowing that He will gives us the words to complete our sentences.

We need Him to be our true hidden desire and our words not to be empty but genuine, by wanting Him more than anything on earth. Allowing Him to take your breath away, while sweeping us off our feet and dancing all night with us. Letting Him be the sweeter than the honeycomb that no other could compare to. We should be falling so deeply in love with Him and loving His Word. I mean how great that would be ladies, when we make God pleased; He in return sends so many blessings to us. He sends so many blessings that we can truly say that He means the world to us and He is our everything. Live your lives to please only Him and love the King whom is the only one worthy of such honor and praise.

I can finally say that I have allowed Him to be the true love of my life. He told me months in the process that I finally had fell in love with Him. I am always amazed when He noticed my growth and that it is genuine and sincere for Him. What better man to fall for, than the best one there is? Fall in love with God first, and will see that you are free from disappointment and unrealistic expectations. There are no limits with God. Fall in love with Him, besides He is already in love with you. God is a true gentleman that knows how to treat a lady.

In this season I have actually learned that God can really be what you want and need Him to be. He has been my provider, deliverer, and so amazing to me. In each season in my life I can look back and I was either speechless or in awe about HIM. There is no one, no man, and no person that can take the place that the Lord has in my heart. I am so in love with HIM and I see HIM for who He truly is. This is not a feeling that I developed because of what I heard but something that I have experience. There is an intense level of intimacy in which He keeps sweeping me off my feet and taking my breath away. The beautiful thing is that there is no question on the depths of His love because there are no limits. I know that He loves me so much that I am always expecting great things from Him.

You should continually praise and worship HIM in spirit and in truth. Live your life to please Him and honor Him. Think and spend every single moment with HIM and be not separated from HIM. Let Him be your rock and watch Him to make your heart beat and my blood flow. He completes me and makes me whole. He will accept you for who you are and encourage you to grow. With Him you are never alone. He always knows the right thing to say in the right timing, how amazing is His sweet name Jesus. You can never disturb

Falling for Him

His sleep because He never gets tired of your personality, your voice, or bored with how you look.

The Lord just keeps on loving on you and you can experience something so pure and rich when you just crave HIM more and expect more. You think you know Him but then He shows you another side of HIM and you fall in love all over again. Only Jesus can make you feel this way. Only Jesus can be this intriguing, this interesting and this worthy, only HIM, not a man, only HIM. I love that sweet name and this man you can share because with Him there is so much love. Your love for God and His love for you is what will draw others.

I remember when I fell for God. It was attending church revival. I recall rushing to get to church an hour early in order to get a good seat. Being there for five hours and wanting more of HIM. I was putting on my best for HIM. I anticipated the time I would be with HIM again. Not to see what He said to me but to all my brothers and sisters in Christ. Every night I thirsted more and more. Though the revival was five hours long during the work week I remained attentive for the entire time. Little did I know that I was falling head over heels in love with the one and only, "The King." I use to say that I was a queen waiting for my king but I cannot even give that title to a man, only to the Heavenly Father and I await my prince.

PRAYER
Falling for HIM

Lord I pray that your daughters will have the beautiful opportunity to first fall in love with you. Let them see exactly how special and great you are. Let them know with you there is perfect love. Let them know that falling for you is the best feeling that they can experience in their lives.
AMEN-so be it

PRAISE & WORSHIP
Scriptures

I WILL praise You, O Lord, with my whole heart; I will show forth (recount and tell aloud) all Your marvelous works and wonderful deeds! Psalm 9:1

I WILL bless the Lord at all times; His praise shall continually be in my mouth. Psalm 34:1

PRAISE THE Lord! (Hallelujah!) O give thanks to the Lord, for He is good; for His mercy and loving-kindness endure forever!   Psalm 106:1

Those who reverently and worshipfully fear You will see me and be glad, because I have hoped in Your word and tarried for it. Psalm 119:74

A time will come, however, indeed it is already here, when the true (genuine) worshipers will worship the Father in spirit and in truth (reality); for the Father is seeking just such people as these as His worshipers. John 4:23

God is a Spirit (a spiritual Being) and those who worship Him must worship Him in spirit and in truth (reality). John 4:24

And He has put a new song in my mouth, a song of praise to our God. Many shall see and fear (revere and worship) and put their trust and confident reliance in the Lord. Psalm 40:3

The reverent fear and worship of the Lord is the beginning of Wisdom and skill [the preceding and the first essential, the prerequisite and the alphabet]; a good understanding, wisdom, and meaning have all those who do [the will of the Lord]. Their praise of Him endures forever. [Job. 28:28; Prov. 1:7; Matt. 22:37, 38; Rev. 14:7.] Psalm 111:10

CHAPTER 4

Following His Purpose

When you submit to His purpose and His will, your life begins. As I have stated before, God is a gentlemen. His Word states in Revelation 3:20, "Behold, I stand at the door and knock; if anyone listens to and heeds My voice and opens the door, I will come in to him and will eat with him, and he [will eat] with Me. He is looking for us to be willing to submit. When we say yes with our heart, mind, and soul then we can do His will. He needs us to build up His Kingdom, to be representations of HIM, and a living testimony in which our lives are real evidence of His true Word.

This is a *Love Letter* from the Father. The love letters are in several of the chapters and they are inspired by God. He revealed this during my prayer time by the way of the Holy Spirit. This was a beautiful experience and I was amazed what He had to say to His daughters.

Dear Daughter,
Go as you are instructed- the correct way is to be submitted unto me. When you are submitted to me that is when my Will will be done. You must first submit yourself unto me. True submission is what is required of you. Then you will develop yourself for my purpose. Then revelation comes,–

doors open, and even windows. What do I have to say unto you? Miracles will be performed right before your eyes. (Oh my sisters watch and see Him transform you for His purpose). Correction comes when following my purpose; discipline comes and self control comes when following my purpose. You will not be hindered by emotions or mental diseases, for I am greater than anything. Believe what I say unto you. You listen unto me. I speak clear to you. I speak to man's heart. I work on changing the way you perceive things and the way you view things of this world. This world is temporary and all aspects and the only thing that is permanent is me.

You look unto me for help, I am your source. Your concentration should be on me and not what is said to you but what I say to you. I say unto you cross over the bridge to get to the other side. I already, already, have a plan for you. You walk in victory! You walk…you walk…you walk with your head up! You walk with prosperity. My purpose for your life is for you to be complete, you be complete in me. You walk and you go . I have so much planned for you. All I ask of you is to seek me with all of your heart. Seek me with a pure heart and love me. I say unto you love me… love me, for love is so great to my purpose. So great to my purpose and for you to seek me and I can give you great rest. Reside in me permanently.

(The utterance of the Spirit continues…)

No greater love… No greater love. Your Father loves you so much. All the pains that have pulled you away from me, peace come and replace these things. For they are temporary; distractions. Temporary it is a state of mind. But you walk in and live in my glory, because you are one of mine that I have chosen. You are the one that I have chosen and I do not make mistakes. I selected you for fulfilling my purpose. Will you accept? Will you accept me? Will you accept my invitation with all your heart? Will you let me flood your heart? Will you accept? Do you hear me? Are you open to me or are you close to me? Ask me. Come all the way to me. Walk to me and I welcome you. I stand and I wait with open arms. My arms are stretched forward to reach you. You do not have to cry I have forgiven you for all of your sin and transgressions. I have forgiven you. I see you as a great flower. I see you so great. I see you and you are beautiful to me. You are my work of art. Allow me to add those finishing touches. Allow me to let your light shine how I attended it to be. Allow me to walk with you. Allow me to guide you. Allow me to reveal to you my purpose for your life, but know all (everything) goes back unto me. Hear me, your daddy's voice; hear me because I know you and I hear your struggles and pains. I cast down pain and misery living. Misery living is not same as sufferings; it is not the same as identical sufferings. Identical sufferings are not designed to break you down but to build you up to my purpose. Some things you go through are not a part of your destiny. Is not a part of my plan. It is not a part at all. So do not believe false teachings. You believe me. You have to study me. You learn me in order to know me authentically. You have to embrace me to know my touch and my voice. Sweet girl, you must know my touch and not mans.

    Be intimate with me and that is what will change your life and your perspective. It is so beautiful when you walk with me. I promise you, when you walk for my purpose for your life. Your Heavenly Father waits that day when his children return from a long journey. (All roads lead to home; to heaven, all roads leads to the same designation, all roads lead to HIM) You go! You go! I know my daughter; greater rewards await you and know that according to my purpose. Oh! Know that I called you for the building of my Kingdom. Seek me to learn your role and your purpose. There is no need of a plan without the purpose. People lose faith and they lose hope when direction cannot be found, cannot be determine, or they cannot understand the purpose. Are good things true favor? Are miracles true favor? Miracles will manifest in the natural for my purpose only, not for your glory. There is no glory in man but only in the Father.

My child you always stay humble. It is important that you do not boast yourself up in this season. Do not prop yourself up but stay humble. Humility that is the way you should be. That is what souls (people) are drawn to, humble leadership people, that have people in the WOW factor. They say, "WOW! He seems so humble to be a leader, he must love God." You must have a servant's attitude and you must reside in the Father. Walk in love without judging but loving and helping others in their time of need.

Love God

What a great God we must serve for we truly have been taught.

PRAYER
Following His Purpose

    Lord I pray that my sisters submit to your will and follow you in all areas of their lives. Teach them submission Father and let them be cheerful while doing so. Lord I pray that your grace and mercy fills my sisters' lives and that they learn your purpose and they do their part to build up your kingdom.
    AMEN, so be it.

DESTINY
Scriptures

No, God has not rejected and disowned His people [whose destiny] He had marked out and appointed and foreknown from the beginning. Do you not know what the Scripture says of Elijah, how he pleads with God against Israel? Romans 11:2

And when the Gentiles heard this, they rejoiced and glorified (praised and gave thanks for) the Word of God; and as many as were destined (appointed and ordained) to eternal life believed (adhered to, trusted in, and relied on Jesus as the Christ and their Savior). Acts 13:48

For those whom He foreknew [of whom He was aware and loved beforehand], He also destined from the beginning [foreordaining them] to be molded into the image of His Son [and share inwardly His likeness], that He might become the firstborn among many brethren. Romans 8:29

So that we who first hoped in Christ [who first put our confidence in Him have been destined and appointed to] live for the praise of His glory! Ephesians 1:12

Urged on] by faith Abraham, when he was called, obeyed and went forth to a place which he was destined to receive as an inheritance; and he went, although he did not know or trouble his mind about where he was to go. Hebrews 11:8

For He foreordained us (destined us, planned in love for us) to be adopted (revealed) as His own children through

Following His Purpose

Jesus Christ, in accordance with the purpose of His will [because it pleased Him and was His kind intent]—Ephesians 1:5

And I asked, what shall I do, Lord? And the Lord answered me, Get up and go into Damascus, and there it will be told you all that it is destined and appointed for you to do. Acts 22:10

And he said, The God of our forefathers has destined and appointed you to come progressively to know His will [to perceive, to recognize more strongly and clearly, and to become better and more intimately acquainted with His will], and to see the Righteous One (Jesus Christ, the Messiah), and to hear a voice from His [own] mouth and a message from His [own] lips; Acts 22:14

Will You Marry Me?

CHAPTER 5

Understanding His Design

God's design was to reconcile us back to Him. Because of sin we were separated from the Father. Oh He loved us so much that He sent His son Jesus to die for us to pay for the penalty of Adam's sin. That is when the original sin stepped in place, Adam's disobedience. God wants all His children to come back to Him; that is His ultimate purpose for our lives. Everything leads us back to Him and to be in right standing with Him.

Once you spend time with Him, you learn Kingdom. As you learn Kingdom, you learn the principles that go with it.

Love Letter

Dear Daughter,
They need corrections from false teaching, false hope, and false promises. Where did this originate from? Where does it come from? It comes from the evil one. My design is to be understood. It is simple for every man to understand. My design is a simple one. Adam was my first son but he broke the covenant. When Adam listened to the evil one, he broke the covenant. So I had already had a plan for my children to come back to me. I sent the best part of me; my

son was a part of me. I could not have designed it any better. However, with Adam sin set forth evil, evil could not produce good but more evil and sin brought more sin. I bring forth life through my Son. My design is that man returns to the covenant with me. Sin separated us and broke the covenant. So I had to send Jesus for the sake of all sinners. That penalty has been paid in full for you. You are free from bondage through Him. My son reunites us together. My desire is for you to return home to me. My desire is for no man to perish and that no man feels the permanent separation from me. I love you so much.

Oh! The time will come that the world will not be. I don't want to lose one. I love all of my children. All of you I love, all of you. I don't want to lose one of my sheep. I want all of you to come home. I have waited for decades and centuries for that to occur but I know that I must honor my word. Oh my daughter, I cannot force myself on you. I speak to but you must hear me. Oh my child I want that covenant with man to be restored and to be reconciled with me. Sin came and broke that covenant but my design is for you to come back to me. My purpose, design, and plan are for you return to me. Oh return home. As you read this book, know in your heart that I am your Father.

Know that I design you in image of me. Just be what I called you to be. Have a repenting heart, so I can work through you for you. But know that my design is simple, it is so simple. My love is not complicated. The way I love you is more than you can ever imagine. Oh my dear love, you will know in this new. You feel this love over take you. So my design is for you and yours to return to me. Know the importance of this and know the truth. Do not be deceived by man's false teachings. Know my design is for you to connect back to me. Know that I care for you affectionately. Know you are mine. Sin will take no place in heaven and has already been paid for and atoned for. Know that just as I

Understanding His Design

designed an out for the recklessness sin of Adam, I provided and an out for every circumstance or encounter. There is an out and that out is Jesus.

Seek me and study the way He lived. Interact the way He did and serve me. Study Jesus, the book of Matthew speaks of Him but know that I spoke of Him throughout the entire word. I knew the fall of man would be great but because I am great, I sent Jesus to reconcile that great sin in deed. Again, know that I have an out for every situation or circumstance that you may or have faced. I am stronger than any force of evil that attempts to prevail against you.

Know that I am God, the Alpha and Omega, the beginning and the end. I am the Great I am. I am the Prince of Peace. I am the buckler. I am the top of the mountains. I am the wind that blows. I am the sky. I am whatever you need me to be. I am the confidant. I am the comforter. I am your friend. I am your Husband. I am the Great I am, all by myself. For I, AM God.

PRAYER
Understanding His Design

    Lord I pray that my sisters in Christ understand your design for their lives, but most important your ultimate design for all of your children lives. Let them follow your map and outlines that you have them follow.
    AMEN, so be it.

HIS DESIGN
Scriptures

And [He designed] to reconcile to God both [Jew and Gentile, united] in a single body by means of His cross, thereby killing the mutual enmity and bringing the feud to an end. Ephesians 2:16

We are assured and know that [God being a partner in their labor] all things work together and are [fitting into a plan] for good to and for those who love God and are called according to [His] design and purpose. Romans 8:28

In Him we also were made [God's] heritage (portion) and we obtained an inheritance; for we had been foreordained (chosen and appointed beforehand) in accordance with His purpose, Who works out everything in agreement with the counsel and design of His [own] will, Ephesians1:11

But that when the days come when the trumpet call of the seventh angel is about to be sounded, then God's mystery (His secret design, His hidden purpose), as He had announced the glad tidings to His servants the prophets, should be fulfilled (accomplished, completed). Revelation 10:7

[And this He will do] provided that you continue to stay with and in the faith [in Christ], well-grounded and settled and steadfast, not shifting or moving away from the hope [which rests on and is inspired by] the glad tidings (the Gospel), which you heard and which has been preached [as being designed for and offered without restrictions] to every person under heaven, and of which [Gospel] I, Paul, became a minister. Colossians 1:23

Now we recognize and know that the Law is good if anyone uses it lawfully [for the purpose for which it was designed], 1 Timothy 1:8

For Christ is the end of the Law [the limit at which it ceases to be, for the Law leads up to Him Who is the fulfillment of its types, and in Him the purpose which it was designed to accomplish is fulfilled. That is, the purpose of the Law is fulfilled in Him] as the means of righteousness (right relationship to God) for everyone who trusts in and adheres to and relies on Him. Romans 10:4

CHAPTER 6

Revelation

God wants to reveal His plan for you. God gives us all gifts and the ability to understand Him. He gives us visions, dreams, and discovery of His hidden word. The power of meditating on His word day and night gives you so many advantages of knowing His plan for your life. When spiritual revelations come, it lines up with His Word. It is sort of like checks and balances. Out of all things that God has told me, I am still like "wow" it actually lines up with His word. I am so amazed that He speaks to me so clearly and I am puzzled and cautious. I never want to lie and say that He has said something He did not in deed state. I know His voice because I spend time with Him daily.

When He reveals, He does not only reveal things about you but also about others. He spoke so many things about others in my prayer time that I cannot even recall it all.

Love Letter

Dear Daughter,
I will reveal things to them but they must know me for that to happen. Revelation is hidden wisdom and knowledge that is given by God and inspired by the Holy Spirit. Your revelation comes to you, to direct you to where you must go.

Will You Marry Me?

You understand my words and my truths. My words and truths are life. Revelations comes in many ways. My ways are not man's ways. My ways are unique and define accordingly to my overall purpose for my Kingdom.

My Kingdom is a place for the rest of my heirs. They are Kingdom heirs. They are to walk in Kingdom. Kingdom living is prosperity and that is more than material possessions. Kingdom living is when you have peace in the greatest storm but you yet not waver or wonder whose you are.

You know you can rely confidently on me. You rely on the word already spoken. Your trust is so great and so deep that you never move. You never deny my works or my capabilities. You declare to the end of this world that I am God. You declare that wisdom is in you. You reject changing when the wind blows but you stand firm on my promises. You stand on my promises that I have said because you believe in the true revelation of my son. You see vivid images of stories told in my Word and you have dreams that tell how the story plays out.

I perform miracles every single day even though you do not realize that I do. I make the blind see across the world. Miracles happen daily. There are people who pray daily with sincere hearts and I answered them. There are children that talk to me daily and worship me in spirit and truth. They praise me constantly and honor me and I answer their prayers. All nationalities do I govern. All that serves me and worships me in spirit and in truth, I answer their prayers. You may not know all the cancers that I have healed and cast down to hell. You may not know all I have made walk. I affect lives in various capacities. You may not know all who I protect. I protect girls from kidnappers and families from burglaries in neighborhood. I am forever and therefore I am infinite. I am everywhere at all times. I am the only one who knows all about my children. I am that one who hears and honor prayers of the righteous. I am the only one who

Revelation

determines solutions and perform great miracles always for those who truly serve and those who have great faith.

You that have an ear let them hear me and trust me. You that seek me come and walk with me and I will show you what I have for you to see. Walk with me and I will reveal to you clearer and ask me for understanding. You ask me then I will tell and instruct you. I will, why would I not? Know that I am God and that I love you so much. Know that He waits on that map but if you do not listen you may miss the perfect connection I have for the both of you my daughter. Grasp me and grasp my revelation. My love is so pure so sweet. When love is done the way that I design it to be, you can expect great things. I have always answered prayers and I have always revealed to my children. I have always been there and will be there. I am God in many places, all at the same time. Everywhere you look and ever where you go I am there.

My works speaks for themselves, if you are ready to know a revelation is being imparted into you right now. Know that the things concerning your life I have made an out for you but you must walk it out. You must practice my principles faithfully. You be faithful and be steadfast. Plant seed in good ground and watch the harvest I have for you. Watch the seed multiply to a great harvest to take care of you and your family and all that is connected to you. You will be blessed by the seed that you have planted. You must plant in good ground. You must nurture that seed with prayer, fasting, and have faith that the seed will grow into a harvest in due season.

You must be like a farmer overseeing his work. For he makes sure that he waters and fertilizes at the right time. He cares for his crop, for he knows what his rewards are. He knows the profit that his crop will bring. He cares for his crop such as you must care for the word that has been implanted in you. You must care for the word that I implanted in you. You must water it daily or the word will surely die. You must know what types of fertilizers to apply, so that can foster the change you want to see.

Wisdom is what my children need to know in order to know how to apply and when to apply. I will lead you on and instruct you on how to do these things. This is a personal conversation we must have daily. How can I reveal when you are not there to seek after me? How can I guide you when you are not in position for these things and instructions? You must be there for me to develop you. You need to be an effective listener and know my voice. You must know I am your father. You must know of my wisdom that is spoken in proverbs. You must know my wisdom is great.

You must know my ways and they must become your ways. My ways are not hatred that is man's way no grudge holding, are not my ways. Lust is not my way but love is my way. Deceit is not my ways but honor and integrity are my ways. You must come to know who I am so you can know who you belong to. Without the work and time you will not receive or see the results of your labor. There are many farmers that oversee their crop properly and they received no reward.

You may wonder how do I become a wife and how do I get a husband? You may wonder these things. You are mine, first, I am a jealous God and you will not put anything ahead of me. I must have your mind and soul and your spirit belonging to me. You are mine and I am yours. You must know this and you must love me with all of yourself and have a clear heart or you will not see the crop of a great love mate. Don't you know that I understand your desire? Don't you know I understand that you want help but I am your source? Know that I am your source, not man. No matter how great I made him in the likeness of me, I Am the real thing.

I am what your heart craves. I am that companion that you long for. I am that intimacy you desire. I am that Alpha

Revelation

and Omega. I am the beginning and the end. I am, I am God. Know me, get to know me and put things in perspective. You are not supposed to lose yourself. You are to complete my plan and my purpose. Child hear me, I know your patience and impatience ways. I know the holes and voids in your heart. I know you're dreadful past sufferings but man cannot fix what he did not break.

Come meet a King, so I can heal you. The one who can deliver you and who loves you so much more, come and meet me. Return to me my sweet daughter. Return to me and walk with me. Worship me and rely on me and I promise that I will give you a greater gift than you ever imagined. I promise I will reveal to you the greater tomorrow right before your eyes. I am the road map that leads to your destiny. Your journey was designed by me. Do not fall prey to the detours and delays in the road. Do not fall for delays for your destiny awaits you. Do not fall for the lust of the flesh but pray. I will provide you with a comforter.

Love God

PRAYER
Revelation

    Lord I pray that revelation comes to my sisters immediately and that they will know that it is your voice that they are to follow. Let them be able to have much spiritual understanding and wisdom that they know how to keep their souls in right standing with you.
    AMEN, so be it.

REVELATION
Scriptures

Happy (blessed, fortunate, enviable) is he who has the God of [special revelation to] Jacob for his help, whose hope is in the Lord his God. Psalm 146:5

Blessed (happy, enviably fortunate, and spiritually prosperous--possessing the happiness produced by the experience of God's favor and especially conditioned by the revelation of His grace, regardless of their outward conditions) are the pure in heart, for they shall see God! Matthew 5:8

But the natural, non-spiritual man does not accept or welcome or admit into his heart the gifts and teachings and revelations of the Spirit of God, for they are folly (meaningless nonsense) to him; and he is incapable of knowing them [of progressively recognizing, understanding, and becoming better acquainted with them] because they are spiritually discerned and estimated and appreciated.1 Corinthians 2:14

[Things are hidden temporarily only as a means to revelation.] For there is nothing hidden except to be revealed, nor is anything [temporarily] kept secret except in order that it may be made known. Mark 4:22

Now, brethren, if I come to you speaking in [unknown] tongues, how shall I make it to your advantage unless I speak to you either in revelation (disclosure of God's will to man) in knowledge or in prophecy or in instruction?1 Corinthians 14:6

Will You Marry Me?

[THIS IS] the revelation of Jesus Christ [His unveiling of the divine mysteries]. God gave it to Him to disclose and make known to His bond servants certain things which must shortly and speedily come to pass in their entirety. And He sent and communicated it through His angel (messenger) to His bond servant John, Revelation 1:1

Behold, [in the future restored Jerusalem] I will lay upon it health and healing, and I will cure them and will reveal to them the abundance of peace (prosperity, security, stability) and truth. Jeremiah 33:6

But it is from Him that you have your life in Christ Jesus, Whom God made our Wisdom from God, [revealed to us a knowledge of the divine plan of salvation previously hidden, manifesting itself as] our Righteousness [thus making us upright and putting us in right standing with God], and our Consecration [making us pure and holy], and our Redemption [providing our ransom from eternal penalty for sin]. 1 Corinthians 1:30

CHAPTER 7

Hope to My Sisters

The Holy Spirit will guide you. The Holy Spirit led me to attend marriage ministry, last session, for the year. This marriage ministry was dynamic; it was done by an Elder couple, who had true passion for encouraging couples in their union. These sessions allowed marriage couples to discuss issues and challenges faced but with spiritual resolutions.

I had not gone before because although I was legally married, I knew my marriage had been dissolved. However, this time I knew I needed to be there. I believed that God was developing me and showing me how to make a marriage work. This was a part of the process and I attended.

One of my sisters in Christ went with me and we were both blessed. I gained insight on how God wanted me to be in a marriage and what He expected from my husband to be. Though the panel was excellent, I got more out of a pamphlet that I picked up during the intermission.

I remember the first time the Holy Spirit led me to pray for my new husband. I did not want to because I had the best from God. I couldn't bring myself to truly focus on my new husband besides who could compare to God. Though I was reluctant I was obedient and He spoke that He was preparing my new husband for his next. God spoke on the qualities that my husband was going to have in Him. Being selfish, I asked the Lord didn't He want me to pray for myself? However, I continued to pray for my husband and then I was led to pray for myself.

During prayer that night God told me He could finally trust me. He shared that He wanted me this way since my college years. I remember being so intimate with Him in college but I turned away because of distraction of wanting a man. It had been prophesized to me that every time God tried to have my attention I went to another man. Though I heard the prophecy, I continued searching for love from a man. Now ten years later, God was saying that He could trust me. He instructed me to be the bold woman of God that He called me to be and that it was time for me to take my place. God stated that I needed to watch the Holy Spirit roar up in me like never before. It then happened, the Lord told me that I was released to speak and declare things about my new husband. He told me that I had finally had fallen in love with HIM (God) first.

I could not get excited at first about a new husband. I cannot explain it but I did not trust myself to love again. I did not want to make the same mistake twice and I did not want to damage another one of God's sons; I could not do that again. The Lord showed me that I was fearful and I casted it down. I went forward and it was so beautiful because He released it for my sisters all over and I finally could enjoy the conversation but this time I kept it in perspective and was led by the Holy Spirit, not my desires. I went to the bridal salon with no intentions to try on a dress, but I did and actually had tears.

For the next several days after that I was released to share the news with friends. Little did I know that they experienced the same unction as well. I received a text message telling me to call a number for prayer and prophecy but I did not have a desire to call. The next day I awoke and had a vision of my bridesmaids' dresses and before I didn't even have a desire for a second wedding. Now I could see the dresses, I then sent out a text and declared that the New Year was going to be great and how we were going to be new. I declared that we were going to have men who loved God more than anything and that they would be men of integrity. I declared that they would know how to love us the way God intended. Shortly after, I received a response from one of my friends about the prophecy text the night before; I got a new text stating that I must have gotten on the call. I spoke to my friend that morning and she explained that the call was speaking about how God was going to send Christian men to Christian women and I got the chills. I was having this conversation for a couple of days and now I knew that I could be excited. I was not anxious and that day I fell more in love with God because I did not become distracted and I was learning how to love, how He wanted me to love.

My pastor preached that following Sunday about loving the Lord, and having a balance. He discussed being submitted to your husband and how He needs to be submitted to the pastor who submitted to God.

Though I have hope and am excited I keep in mind that His Word says to be anxious for nothing and to not be consumed. Yes, I am happy that I can remarry but on earth it is important, in heaven it does not exist. So I am enjoying life while I am here on earth but my primary focus is on the Father and spending my eternity with HIM (God- MY first and my last true Husband).

My sister in Christ had shared that it had been put on her heart to have a New Years Eve gathering for all the singles. So we would not have to bring in the New Year alone. Life is truly how you perceive things and that night we looked at the glass half full. We were not sad or complaining but we rejoiced, had fun and spoke on great things to come. We talked about our new unions and we danced as if it was our wedding day. It was beautiful and hopeful. We were women of different walks of life but all in our late 20's and 30's filled with joy and expectation of the Father. We bought the New Years in praying and praising. Christian women waiting on our Father to send men that He had designed for us in the beginning.

Though we all had made mistakes our sins were all covered with His blood. God tells that we can have what we ask, if we forgive… that is the key we must forgive others and be in position to receive what He has for us. Though fear tries to come back, I know that I can talk to Daddy and that He will restore my hope. Bitterness is not of Him; we must learn to let go and face our fears. We must first allow ourselves to be vulnerable to the Father. Then we can be confident and know that He gives us, our heart desires.

Two months later God instructed me to write about my husband. I did not fear and I was hopeful. When fear is present and faith cannot be activated fully, in its proper place. I was uncomfortable when God showed me; I tried to deny it and became apprehensive. I could not believe that I was afraid because I trusted God. But God showed me the reason I could not get excited on a constant basis was because of the fear. He told me to look up apprehensive and I did, though I had dressed it up with another name the meaning was fear. I was out done, God loves us so much that He wants us to repent and be whole in all areas so that He can give us what He has for us. Yes, it was uncomfortable and painful to deal with but I am thankful that He loves me so much that He did not want the fear I had of a man to stop loving me to block the great man, He has for me.

I write this section with the unction of the Holy Spirit. Marriage is one of the things that I focus on doing God's way. Though I hope for a second wedding, ultimately I hope to always be strong in faith, wise and patient and to take care of the gift that God gives me. I must know the power of prayer and power of confessing God's Words and expecting them to come to pass. The wedding day is the easy part. The marriage is where the work comes, in and full time work is an understatement. The flow can be easy if you both follow the Holy Spirit and not your flesh. I have yet to be married the way God intended it to be. Though this will not be my first marriage, it will be a new experience because I have been changed.

I am definitely not the same person I once was; I am confident and wiser now. I know how to fight and resist, the devil and he will flee. His Word states and that is what I declared was mine and I will not stay frustrated and sad when situations arise but, to fight the good fight of Faith. We can win if we stay constantly rooted in Him and seek HIM in all things by being led.

To my sister you are released to have hope. If you try to live by His word, His truth and do His will, His principles will work. Honor God and hope is right around the corner. Honor, healing, and hope all go in a certain order. When we honor Him, He then heals us and restores hope to us, what a good God we serve. Once again we must forgive, it is essential for our healing process. We must honor God, it keeps us in perspective and we must hope because it eliminates fears. That hope brings forth miracles and blessings, all the time God gets the glory. We have the opportunity to work together to build the Lord's Kingdom.

Oh! To be a part of something as great as saving souls and watching them return to our Heavenly Father. So I plea with you don't give up on your dreams and your desires, just put God first and keep marriage in God's perspective. Have a true desire to know HIM and hope for His knowledge and then no good thing will be withheld from you. Sisters know that God knows your heart, ask Him to purge your heart and make you in right standing with Him. Seek wisdom through praying and fasting and He will give you the desire to hunger more for His word. Love, hope, and trusting are all a part of learning Him and knowing who He is.

God is compassionate and He does not desire for you to be alone. However, you must first be completely satisfied with HIM. You must want Him more than anything. Then when you least expect Him, the Lord will give you someone that on your best day you could not even imagine. He will give you a mate to compliment you not to complete you because He has done that already. He will give you someone you can encourage and that encourages you to walk in love and speak in love. Trust God and He will guide you. Listen to His voice and look to Him for understanding and He will answer you.

PRAYER
Hope to My Sisters

    Lord, I pray that you will restore hope where there has been pain, doubt, and bitterness. Lord, heal them. I declare they are free from the past and healed from its scares. Let the scares be only a reminder of your grace and mercy. Bitterness has no place in your Kingdom and it has no place in their lives. With hope comes healing and with healing comes more hope. Let my sisters in Christ expect great things from you. Lord let them dream again. Lord let them love the way you designed them to love their husbands'. And Lord let their husbands love them the way you loved the church.
    AMEN, so be it.

ENCOURAGING
Scriptures

I have seen that everything [human] has limits and end [no matter how extensive, noble, and excellent]; but your commandment is exceedingly broad and extends without limits [into eternity] [Rom. 3:10-19.] Psalm 119:96

Then she came and told the man of God. He said, Go, sell the oil and pay your debt, and you and your sons live on the rest. II Kings 4:7

For whatever was thus written in former days was written for our instruction, that by [our steadfast and patient] endurance and the encouragement [drawn] from the Scriptures we might hold fast to and cherish hope. Romans 15:4

For the eyes of the Lord are upon the righteous (those who are upright and in right standing with God), and His ears are attentive to their prayer. But the face of the Lord is against those who practice evil [to oppose them, to frustrate, and defeat them]. 1 Peter 3:12

David was greatly distressed, for the men spoke of stoning him because the souls of them all were bitterly grieved, each man for his sons and daughters. But David encouraged and strengthened himself in the Lord his God. 1 Samuel 30:6

Who comforts (consoles and encourages) us in every trouble (calamity and affliction), so that we may also be able to comfort (console and encourage) those who are in any kind of trouble or distress, with the comfort (consolation and encouragement) with which we ourselves are comforted (consoled and encouraged) by God. 2 Corinthians 1: 4

You have loved righteousness [You have delighted in integrity, virtue, and uprightness in purpose, thought, and action] and You have hated lawlessness (injustice and iniquity). Therefore God, [even] Your God (Godhead), has anointed You with the oil of exultant joy and gladness above and beyond Your companions. Hebrews 1:9

And the harvest of righteousness (of conformity to God's will in thought and deed) is [the fruit of the seed] sown in peace by those who work for and make peace [in themselves and in others, that peace which means concord, agreement, and harmony between individuals, with undisturbedness, in a peaceful mind free from fears and agitating passions and moral conflicts]. James 3:18

[After all] the kingdom of God is not a matter of [getting the] food and drink [one likes], but instead it is righteousness (that state which makes a person acceptable to God) and [heart] peace and joy in the Holy Spirit. Romans 14:17

Wait and hope for and expect the Lord; be brave and of good courage and let your heart be stout and enduring. Yes, wait for and hope for and expect the Lord. Psalms 27:14

Rejoice and exult in hope; be steadfast and patient in suffering and tribulation; be constant in prayer. Romans 12:12

But I will hope continually, and will praise You yet more and more. Psalms 71:14

But those who wait for the Lord [who expect, look for, and hope in Him] shall change and renew their strength and power; they shall lift their wings and mount up [close to God] as eagles [mount up to the sun]; they shall run and not be weary, they shall walk and not faint or become tired. Isaiah 40:31

Hope deferred makes the heart sick, but when the desire is fulfilled, it is a tree of life. Proverbs 13:12

When he arrived and saw what grace (favor) God was bestowing upon them, he was full of joy; and he continuously exhorted (warned, urged, and encouraged) them all to cleave unto and remain faithful to and devoted to the Lord with [resolute and steady] purpose of heart. Acts 11:23

CHAPTER 8

Remaining Focused

In the midst of my storms, I had a difficult time staying focused on the Heavenly Father. Even though He told me to stay centered during my personal trials, I was not obedient. My pastor and prayer ministry kept instructing me to hold on to my faith, but it seemed impossible for me to do. I can understand how Peter felt when Jesus asked him to walk on water. Though he answered His request with a "Yes," Peter walked with timid faith and took his eyes off of Jesus and began to drown. I always said that if I were Peter I would not have taken my eyes off of Jesus but, that is because I am in a new day. Even now with a renewed faith I sometimes struggle with remaining steadfast.

Though I am not in Jesus' physical presence, I feel so close to Him in the spirit. How did I take my eyes off the prize? I looked at the circumstances and kept revisiting the past. We are to learn from our past but not relive it. We are to enjoy our new and the promises of God. We should be focused on completing our assignments and walking in our destiny. When you hear His voice, follow Him.

With prayer and practice remaining focused is an area that I have grown in, this last year. I must remain focused on the Father because when you take your eye off of HIM, you open yourself up to fears and anxieties. You begin to believe that you are in the fight alone. We must activate our faith and focus on Christ leading us on where He has for us to go.

There were times that I lost struggle with staying focused because I would take my eyes off the Father during marriage and separation. When I looked at the situation I would become frustrated, angry, and powerless. You cannot win a spiritual war by fighting carnally. You have to be aware of the trick of the enemy to have you in confusion so that he can keep you from the purpose and blessings that await you. You can be so close but if Satan gets you in strife with another person, he has accomplished his goal. Don't give him that power but focus on the Father.

Love Letter

Dear Daughter,
When you trust me, you stay steady. When you keep your eyes solely on me because it is not about what you may see on each side of you. You go when I say go regardless of the obstacles you may face. When you are obedient, you must conform to my ways and not your comforts. Out of your comforts comes distractions and they cause delays and that causes you to lose focus. If you are not careful you will lose your faith.

What is the original thing I said unto you? What did I say to you in the beginning? What did I say to you? Truly believe me, this is not a game of football or a game of soccer. This is not a play or fiction. This is not a story told. This is my truth. You must not take your eyes off me. What must I do to prove that I Am the I Am? What must I do to prove that I turned water into wine? What must I do to get you to understand that I am what I said I am? What must I do to unlock the doors? What must I do to have you surrender to me? What must I do to let you know how much I love you? What must I do to let you know how much I care? Peter walked on water, yes I am the same person who did that but he took his eye off of me. That is when you tell yourself I must stay focused on what He has already said. It does not matter how young you were when I spoke to you. What matters is that I brought it back to your remembrance. What matters is that you knew it was me. What matters is what I actually said to you. What matters is on what you do with the information? The data, is important, will you process the data?

Will you wait until later? Don't delay your destiny. I want you to enjoy it, enjoy me and enjoy your inheritance, not later but now. Hear me! Hear me! I want you to be so happy, far from simple happiness but greater joy that everyone around you. You should have joy and that is where your peers will take a second look. That is where you will find peace but remain focus on me. Keep your eyes locked on me because I do not take my eyes off you. I set my eyes on my children to protect and shield them from the evils of this world. You must hear, you will serve and show honor. Will you love the one who gave His life for you? With an open heart, with an open heart accept me. For I have already accepted you.

Will you love me? Will you be my wife and let me be your husband? Oh! Will you allow me to make you happier than you ever seen? Will you allow me to be intimate with you? Will you allow me to love you, love you not like any other? My love is so great, just keeping your eyes on me and I know I will not take my eyes off of you. I will follow you on your journey because I am making sure you walk in your destiny with confidence and a humble spirit. I am making sure that your heart is always pure, so you can witness to the souls of people. For you are earning great rewards. Learn me; I will make sure that you reach the greater thoughts. I am a loving God. I love all my children. All means everyone.

Will You Marry Me?

Do not let the evil deeds of man take you off course. Stand firm and walk. Do not be tricked by the evil one and conformed to the evil ways. Combat evil. But you're my daughter; you walk in love as I have already told you. You walk in forgiveness and you apply those fruits of the spirit. You apply my principles and watch me. Watch me, and know I would not give you a task I thought or knew you could not complete; a task that was greater than you were capable of. The task can be accomplished, just listen to me and I will direct you.

Keep walking closer to me, where peace is. Come closer to me, come close to me and you will see that the focus becomes easier in time, when you build a greater trust in me. I love you. I love you and know I am love. Love is me and this book is on loving me.

"Will you marry me?" is the question of the hour. Will you marry me? Will you commit, obey, and cherish me? Will you yearn and long for me to walk on the beach that I create? Will you marry me first? Ask yourself, will you? Then everything I have for you, my daughter I will give to you. I wait, I wait for you to make you complete.

Love God

PRAYER
Remaining Focus

Lord I pray that my sisters remain totally focused on you. Lord let them be so in tune with your Holy Spirit that they will not be distracted by trails, tribulations, or the enemy. Let them know if they keep their minds on you that they can do all things through Christ that strengthens them.

AMEN, so be it.

UNMOVEABLE
Scriptures

Withstand him; be firm in faith against his onset-rooted , established, strong , immovable, and determined], knowing that the same identical sufferings ware appointed to your brotherhood (the whole body of Christians) throughout the world. 1 Peter 5:9

Therefore, my beloved brethren, be firm (steadfast), immovable, always abounding in the work of the Lord [always being superior, excelling, doing more than enough in the service of the Lord], knowing and being continually aware that your labor in the Lord is not futile [it is never wasted or to no purpose]. 1 Corinthians 15:58

[And this He will do] provided that you continue to stay with and in the faith [in Christ], well-grounded and settled and steadfast, not shifting or moving away from the hope [which rests on and is inspired by] the glad tidings (the Gospel), which you heard and which has been preached [as being designed for and offered without restrictions] to every person under heaven, and of which [Gospel] I, Paul, became a minister. Colossians 1:23

You know how we call those blessed (happy) who were steadfast [who endured]. You have heard of the endurance of Job, and you have seen the Lord's [purpose and how He richly blessed him in the] end, inasmuch as the Lord is full of pity and compassion and tenderness and mercy. James 5:11

And in [exercising] knowledge [develop] self-control, and in [exercising] self-control [develop] steadfastness (patience, endurance), and in [exercising] steadfastness [develop] godliness (piety), 2 Peter 1:6

Here [comes in a call for] the steadfastness of the saints [the patience, the endurance of the people of God], those who [habitually] keep God's commandments and [their] faith in Jesus. Revelation 14:12

And he shall be like a tree firmly planted [and tended] by the streams of water, ready to bring forth its fruit in its season; its leaf also shall not fade or wither; and everything he does shall prosper [and come to maturity]. Psalm 1:3

Through Him also we have [our] access (entrance, introduction) by faith into this grace (state of God's favor) in which we [firmly and safely] stand. And let us rejoice and exult in our hope of experiencing and enjoying the glory of God. Romans 5:2

Will You Marry Me?

CHAPTER 9

Let Him Be Your Guide

The Lord said that He would not only be with you but also guide you in all areas of your life. The key is to trust and depend on Him. When you love His Word and live upright He will guide you. A good man steps are ordered. Walk in Faith and allow Him to guide you on a smooth path. You will go and your path will be leveled out for you. Walk in – ladies God says to walk in your destiny and watch your life change right before your eyes. Exercise your faith and the Kingdom principles will work for God's glory and for your good. It is like playing follow the leader. Oh! He is a great one to follow; He will guide you on your journey. He will supply you with instructions, directions, and wisdom.

Wisdom comes when you study the Word and through fasting. When you push back the plate and take your primary focus off of things of this world such as food television, entertainment, and other lustful things, then His spirit it is so excellent and so pure. You too can be pure God will reveal and direct you. Follow the flow of God and at heart, as He guides you in the direction He has for you to go. Road map – The Lord's map knows all the pitfalls and detour. He is fully aware of circumstances and the storms that attempt to stop you on your journey and your destiny.

Be a winner and you will definitely be a great finisher. That same excellent spirit that Daddy has we have too, in order to flow with Him. Allow Him to guide you because and He loves you. He prepares you for the trip and He instructs you when to stop and when to go. You will meet so many great people on the road to win souls that will witness to you and you will witness to them. This is a unity concept because we are called to be in unity and harmony with our brothers and sisters.

Love Letter

Dear Daughter,
Oh! There may be detours and they may seem difficult. They may try to take you off course; you press on and go forward. They are designed to protect you while I work things out for your good. I am preparing a perfect fit for you. Only if you trust me for I am God. I know all things about you, every hair on your head. Try me, for you are my child. What greater love does a parent have for their child? Only if you believe in me and the love I have for you. Hold my hand, my dear daughter; walk with me and daughter I will walk with you to a life of success, a life true with pure love, a life of joy and free from agony and free from despair. Free from burdens. You trust me and watch me orchestrate your future. My child you do not always have to understand my ways; lean not on your own understanding. It is imperative that you always trust me. Walk with me and be controlled by my spirit and not your flesh.

In the beginning of life, I breathed life and spirit into man. Return to the simple, the beginning. Trust the one that made you. You will feel the power of me and you will feel my love and my affection for you. Oh! So much love do I have for you. So much knowledge waits for you in order for me to be close to you. Believe me, I made you, in the begin-

ning, I made you the map of success. A map takes you to where you should go and it takes you to purpose. It takes you to the greater plan; it takes you to your destiny. Oh! My child, walk with a friend. That friend being Jesus because He walked first and He knows where the pitfalls are. He makes the walk so perfect for you because He already knows, be in sync with Him. Follow me and follow only me. Rest in me. I designed for you, is a plan smoothly to make it. Go and trust me, your creator, I see all and I know all. My wisdom is infinite. Cool running's, the temperature is set for your journey. *According to Webster, one of the definitions of cool means calm not to be anxious for nothing on this journey we declare and confess that we are not anxious.* The time is right now and you are prepared my beautiful daughter.
    Love God

    I declare that you will trust the Father and let Him be your guide. On our maps the Father has routed our direction in advance, and has made our journey before we were even born. All we have to do is read the map that was prepared for us by Him. God is infinite –endless with no end…

PRAYER
Let HIM be Your Guide

Lord I pray that you guide my sisters' footsteps. Lord I pray that they hear your voice on where you want them to go. Let them know that it is so much bigger than what they see in the natural eye. Let them have that third eye to see in the supernatural. Heavenly Father, let the Holy Spirit led them.
    AMEN, so be it.

BEING GUIDED BY HIM
Scriptures

Guide me in Your truth and faithfulness and teach me, for You are the God of my salvation; for You [You only and altogether] do I wait [expectantly] all the day long. Psalm 25:5

For this God is our God forever and ever; He will be our guide [even] until death. Psalm 48:14

But [God] led His own people forth like sheep and guided them [with a shepherd's care] like a flock in the wilderness. Psalm 78:52

So that the Law served [to us Jews] as our trainer [our guardian, our guide to Christ, to lead us] until Christ [came], that we might be justified (declared righteous, put in right standing with God) by and through faith. Galatians 3:24

But I say, walk and live [habitually] in the [Holy] Spirit [responsive to and controlled and guided by the Spirit]; then you will certainly not gratify the cravings and desires of the flesh (of human nature without God). Galatians 5:16

Now may our God and Father Himself and our Lord Jesus Christ (the Messiah) guide our steps to you. 1Thessalonians 3:11

The integrity of the upright shall guide them, but the willful contrariness and crookedness of the treacherous shall destroy them. Proverbs 11:3

And the Lord shall guide you continually and satisfy you in drought and in dry places and make strong your bones. And you shall be like a watered garden and like a spring of water whose waters fail not. Isaiah 58:11

So [David] was their shepherd with an upright heart; he guided them by the discernment and skillfulness [which controlled] his hands. Psalm 78:72

And He said to them, Come after Me [as disciples--letting Me be your Guide], follow Me, and I will make you fishers of men! Matthew 4:19

CHAPTER 10

Trusting Him

I remember driving to work while I was praying. The Lord spoke to me so clearly and said, "You love me, but you don't trust me." I knew He was telling me the truth but I did not like it because it did not sound good that I did not trust God. Being an analytic person I tried to believe it was not God, but the next song that came on the radio was, "Lord I will trust you," and immediately, I cried out to the Father. It took me a while to learn how to trust Him. I consulted one of my church leaders and she gave me advice but I felt she did not fully understand. I do not know what I expected for the church leader to tell me but I was determined for an answer. So I began to declare and read scriptures on how I could trust Him. I was confident the answer was in the Word but I needed to be sure for myself.

There have been so many blessings that God has done throughout my life. However, I still have to remind myself who God is and trust Him. We tend to look at our own situation in which we are human but we must look at the same picture He sees. Trusting God is an area that I am still working on because Satan would like to plant doubt and defeat us in our heads. That is why it is vital to know the Word for you and know exactly who is without questioning His power. We must know that He is in control at all times and He rules both heaven and earth. At times that can sound far out, but remember when we watched God deliverer us out of situation after situation.

When you think about it, it is so strange how we can trust so many earthly things but do not trust HIM. There are times that we convince ourselves that we depend on Him and know that He can do the impossible. We declare that we rely on only God, but do we speak these things to God in truth? Because when the storm comes we immediately forget who our Savior is and we try to figure out how to solve our problems. That is wavering from believing who He is and His promises. Though it may be difficult to stand when you are faced with major struggles your faith needs to kick in to defeat the enemy.

So trusting God adds up with having faith in God. Knowing once you give it to Him that He is going to work it out for you and at the same time you will be growing in Him and not only will your faith increase but your trust in God.

Love Letter

Dear Daughter
Understand this is a process that you must go through for victory. How can you win the race if you do not run? Trust and know that I am at the beginning of the line and I embrace you at the finish. Quicken your heart to my ways and my knowledge. Humble yourself and see what I have for you. You must see what I have already created for you. It is soon to come, keep trusting in me for the victory. There are rewards so great, something remarkable, something magnificent. Just lean on me, if you lean on me and confide your internal thoughts and your fears then you don't have to tackle them on your own.

Let me do my job in your life do not take on my role. For I am your Father and I take care of you. I love you. You

Trusting Him

trust my voice and my wisdom that I imparted in you. Your wisdom does not compare, you are a little girl ready to explore the world but you must let me develop you for that great journey ahead. The things of this life are what I want for you to enjoy, the things that are of me I want you to have magnificent gifts that await you. There are so many gifts that I have to give to my daughters. You walk in great faith and walk in confidence.

Stay in your true role and keep on rolling with life regardless of what is thrown at you. Continue in spite of the difficulties that you may face for they are temporary diversions of the truth that waits. Be not fooled by the road blocks that come against your success. Be not bewildered of the thoughts of this world but be engaged in me. Be so connected to me that these fall to the waste side. So my child you walk as a Christian woman ought to. You walk with great faith. You follow me, you follow me. Before hand I had an out for you.

In the beginning I knew your purpose for this life and I knew your purpose for this season. I knew where you were going. I knew you before you were in your mother's womb. I knew when you suffered those great things and those things that trouble you until this day. I knew you before there was ever a you, all you must do is get to know me. You must get to be my witness. My powers are so great. You must know that the plan that I need you to create in this time. You go and I will direct and equip you with purpose.

Listen my daughter, listen to me, listen to me. Loving me means you are willing to trust me, walk in those principles, speak in the spirit and confess these things out loud. Go my child, go and you will see that you could have trusted me all the long. You could have experienced the Holy Spirit so much sooner but it is not too late to experience your destiny.

PRAYER
Trusting HIM

    Lord I pray that my sisters trust you. Let them not get in impatient during this process. Let their faith be strengthened daily. Lord, let them continue to praise you regardless of the storms that come. Let their praise and worship increase. Lord let them trust you with their whole heart. Lord let them know that you love them so and that is why they can trust you. Lord increase their patience and joy in this season of trusting you, so peace can come in all their circumstances.
    AMEN, so be it.

Trusting Him

FAITH & TRUST
Scriptures

And Jesus, replying, said to them, Have faith in God [constantly]. Mark 11:22

For this reason I am telling you whatever you ask for in prayer, believe (trust and confident) that it is granted to you and you will [get it] Mark 11:24

And again He says, My trust and assured reliance and confident hope shall be fixed in Him. And yet again, Here I am, I and the children whom God has given Me. [Isa . 8:17, 18.] Hebrews 2:13

Jesus turned around and, seeing her, He said, Take courage, daughter! Your faith has made you well. And at once the woman was restored to health. Matthew 9-22

Then He touched their eyes, saying, According to your faith and trust and reliance [on the power invested in Me] be it done to you; Matthew 9-29

But Jesus said to the woman, Your faith has saved you; go (enter) into peace [in freedom from all the distresses that are experienced as the result of sin]. Luke 7:49-50

And they told the woman, Now we no longer believe (trust, have faith) just because of what you said; for we have heard Him ourselves [personally], and we know that He truly is the Savior of the world, the Christ. John 4:42

So keep up your courage, men, for I have faith (complete confidence) in God that it will be exactly as it was told me; Acts 27:25

But let all those who take refuge and put their trust in You rejoice; let them ever sing and shout for joy, because You make a covering over them and defend them; let those also who love Your name be joyful in You and be in high spirits. Psalm 5:11

As for God, His way is perfect! The word of the Lord is tested and tried; He is a shield to all those who take refuge and put their trust in Him. Psalm 18:30

Trust in, lean on, rely on, and have confidence in Him at all times, you people; pour out your hearts before Him. God is a refuge for us (a fortress and a high tower). Selah [pause, and calmly think of that]! Psalm 62:8

CHAPTER 11

Him Trusting You

The Lord spoke to me that He trusted me, I was like wow! –I was filled with joy on so many other levels, but this was new. God was now telling me that He could trust me. I grab hold to that in all areas of my life, my witness, finances and my relationships with other people are all for the building of His Kingdom. I knew I had grown but I did not expect God to tell me that, I was blown away that day. He has dealt with me in several areas; I promise it is not about me or you it is about his Kingdom being worked and done. It is about your destiny coming to pass. God has a calling and purpose for all His children whom truly seek Him. You should seek God with your whole heart, mind, and soul.

There were so many times that I would go from one relationship to the next because of the need of love and affection that I missed what God was trying to show me. When I was in college, I attended a service in which the pastor prophesied to me that every time God tries to show Himself to me, I go get another man. As I stated before I know this was true but I felt that I needed this love. This sounds odd to me because God is love but why was I still in search for something that was directly in my face. I am so grateful that God was patient with me and He had a work for me to do and loved me in spite of myself. He's just so good like that!

God needs to trust you and know that you love Him more than anything. He must know that you will not let anything separate you from the love that you have for Him. He must be certain that no matter who may leave that you will not turn away from Him but go closer to Him. He is waiting for your prayers to be sincere. When you speak, acknowledge that He is the source. He is waiting on you to be confident in who He is. God wants you to completely trust Him and be able to trust you.

Ladies, God is saying this to us all. That He would like to trust you, so you can experience Him and walk in your purpose that He planned for you in the beginning. Don't allow guilt of the past or present to stop you from the promises that God has for you. You are meant to impact others that you will come in contact with. Therefore, be encouraged ladies because God is waiting.

Love Letter

Dear Daughter,
I have given you the unction of the spirit. This is how I led you. This is how you trust me in every event. There is a certain order that must take place. You may anticipate the speaker or even the song but one will not proceed over the other. Don't miss out but enjoy the remainder of the program because of the anticipation or anxiousness for someone else. Know that every part of the program is critical to your end. Every part plays a role in your story. Every part has a way that led you to trusting me. I am the one who made the plan and the program, most importantly I made you. You are my beautiful princess.

(There is a corresponding link in you trusting Him and Him trusting you. You must understand the process).

I know that you trust me when you fully walk in faith, when I have your heart and your mind. When I know that

Him Trusting You

you put nothing or anyone before me. When our relationship is genuine and real; when your light is kindled by me, only, can you walk with me; when you do my purpose with all your heart. I want to trust you but I must know and be certain that you are ready for the levels of sacrifices that are needed for my plans on earth.

Can I trust you with my souls? Can I trust you to walk in love and be nonjudgmental? Can I trust you to be fair to my children? Can I trust you to truly love your brothers and sisters? Can I trust you to walk in my understanding and not in your own? Can I trust you to love me with all your heart? My daughter there is so much to share in my kingdom. Can I trust you with these blessings? Can I trust you to remain humble and meek? There is a great responsibility that comes with me trusting you. Can you be what I called you to be? Will you submit to my will and my purpose? Will you follow me?

Love God

Though I have faced many sins and temptations, I declare that the Spirit of God in me will govern my life. Until Christ returns, I will serve God and not live lukewarm for the sake of temporary satisfaction of the flesh. My heart will be in a constant and instant state of obedience.

PRAYER
HIM Trusting You

Lord, let us seek you Father with pure hearts. Lord, purge our hearts and show us ourselves so we can repent. Lord we cast down the spirit of pride and we humble ourselves.
AMEN, so be it.

DELIEVENCE & REPENTANCE
Scriptures

And when the Lord saw that they humbled themselves, the word of the Lord came to Shemaiah, saying, they have humbled themselves, so I will not destroy them, but I will grant them some deliverance; and My wrath shall not be poured out upon Jerusalem by the hand of Shishak.   2 Chronicles 12:7

Then you shall see and be radiant, and your heart shall thrill and tremble with joy [at the glorious deliverance] and be enlarged; because the abundant wealth of the [Dead] Sea shall be turned to you, unto you shall the nations come with their treasures.   Isaiah 60:5

Blessed (praised and extolled and thanked) be the Lord, the God of Israel, because He has come and brought deliverance and redemption to His people! Luke 1:68

Besides this you know what [a critical] hour this is, how it is high time now for you to wake up out of your sleep (rouse to reality). For salvation (final deliverance) is nearer to us now than when we first believed (adhered to, trusted in, and relied on Christ, the Messiah). Romans13:11

In Him we have redemption (deliverance and salvation) through His blood, the remission (forgiveness) of our offenses (shortcomings and trespasses), in accordance with the riches and the generosity of His gracious favor, Ephesians 1:7

Bring forth fruit that is consistent with repentance [let your lives prove your change of heart]; Matthew 3:8

For no person will be justified (made righteous, acquitted, and judged acceptable) in His sight by observing the works prescribed by the Law. For [the real function of] the Law is to make men recognize and be conscious of sin [not mere perception, but an acquaintance with sin which works toward repentance, faith, and holy character]. Romans 3:20

THEREFORE LET us go on and get past the elementary stage in the teachings and doctrine of Christ (the Messiah), advancing steadily toward the completeness and perfection that belong to spiritual maturity. Let us not again be laying the foundation of repentance and abandonment of dead works (dead formalism) and of the faith [by which you turned] to God, Hebrews 6:1

The Lord does not delay and is not tardy or slow about what He promises, according to some people's conception of slowness, but He is long-suffering (extraordinarily patient) toward you, not desiring that any should perish, but that all should turn to repentance. 2 Peter 3:9

CHAPTER 12

Purpose: "Freeing Your Mind"

When your mind is free and clear you can see the purpose God has for life. You can see what role you play in building up His Kingdom. You see things the way He intended it to be. What occupies our minds: religion, tradition and our upbringing? We become set in our ways and have a certain interpretation of what we feel we know. Are we oppressed or are we free of our own mentality? How have we learned to cope with life and the stress of life? Is it true that we are heirs of a Great King? Did He come so that we can be free from sin death and have life more abundantly? How do we live this life as a Christian? How do we live this life as a true child of God? How do we walk in the spirit daily? The word clearly states that we are renewed daily. Ephesians states we are to be constantly renewed in the spirit of our minds.

Therefore, God knows that we are faced with daily stressors. He knows that life can take a toll on you. He is aware of the trick of the enemy that comes to distract you and throws you off course. How do we renew our minds daily? We confess and declare that it will be. The word tells us that we are being renewed daily when we activate our faith and allow ourselves to be led by the Holy Spirit. II Corinthians 4 15-17. We become more like our Father and have clothed yourself with the new spiritual self Colossians 3 9-11. The Word also tells us not to be conformed to this world but transformed by the entire renewing of your mind. (Romans 12:1) We are to adapt to God's way of thinking and believe His Word and His principles.

Love Letter

Dear Daughter,
Activate your faith regardless of what the world may say. You activate your faith and read my word. Know my word daily and study my word. Know my word and apply my word. Replace misconceptions and traditions of manmade practices. My ways are for the building of my Kingdom. My goal and purpose is saving all mankind. I need people of constant faith to work my Kingdom's principles, for my work in you can come to pass. I want souls to be saved from destruction. Being separated from me is not what I have for any of my children.

Walk close to me and learn me. It is simple to know me. Yearn for me and a relationship with me. Love me, learn me, trust me and walk with me, my child. I clear clutter; trust me further and other mental disorders that have captivated you for years and generational curses that flowed in your family will leave. You are my family and I am yours, those things that had you in bondage become things of the past. You must know my word to fight these things. You must know but, if you do not spend time with me, you will never know what I have for you. Spend time with me, my daughter. Spend time with me and watch me spend time with you.

Watch me clear your thoughts and watch me work on your behalf. Watch me perform miracles in your life and watch me develop you according to my will. You have no idea how my dreams are for my children. Watch me, a sparkle of hope. There is so much more. Let me mold you.

Purpose: "Freeing Your Mind"

Let me love you. Let me embrace and caress you, oh my dear daughter. My love is so great and full of mercy and grace. Be not deceived of the things of your past because we, the Holy Spirit, the Father, and the Son, we focus on where you are going not where you have been or where you come from. We knew the mistakes that you were going to make but we move you in a progressive state for my name's sake. Take your eyes off your current and your past circumstances and embrace the truth. My ways and my truth is the only way. Believe what I tell you my daughters. Walk with a free mind, free from bondage, and free from the state of mind of oppression. You are free, I sent my Son and I gave Him up in order for the greater good of my children to return to me and to be in my Kingdom.

When this earth passes away, you will be with me. There will be a celebration when my children return home to me. I cannot force you but I ask and I knock. Open your hearts and there are great rewards, benefits and great things. That is, for those who choose me and reject the world. You can only serve one, you cannot serve both. Choose who you will serve, chose me, and chose me. Watch my magnificent works and powers and watch how in a blink of eye I turn things around instantly, so fast that you can even believe it happens so quickly. I can work at any pace that I desire I AM the I AM. All powers belong to me. Know this and change your confessions. Make sure that they line up with my word. What are you speaking? Are you saying what I have said to you? Whose voice do you listen to? Whose voice do you listen to? Hear my voice, your Father's voice? You hear my voice and no other voice will you follow. You hear my voice on this day. Things come to you so much clearer, in the process of me molding such a change on the inside. You will not be conformed of this world, but will be transformed for me and for my glory. For my purpose and my plan because I am your father and you will be my daughter that I called you to be. But know I will not force myself on you, I am a gentleman. I am a gentleman. I am love. I am love and that is all natural, all natural and an easy flow. Listen to me, my daughter, my yoke is easy. Cast your cares on me for I love you. I love you and I adore you, my daughter I adore you my precious daughter and I love you. I cannot say enough, I want you to feel my love so genuinely and unconditionally not expecting anything in return but your love for me in return. Remember and know that my love is natural and it is simple, my sweet daughter. Be the princess that I called you to be and do not let my sufferings be in vain. Let your mind be renewed and be transformed. Listen to me, my words, and my love… my love.

Oh my dear, be fruitful, as well and you love one another as I have loved you. Love beats evil any day, believe me. I have poured out that love in you, so be loving my Christian daughter. Be as I am, love and watch the change that I do. Believe these things to be my daughter and seek wisdom and I will give it you. I will prepare you for the obstacle courses. Love will prepare you for what lies ahead. Love will prepare you for my purpose and my plan for your life. Love is such a great thing and love is so pure. It is so pure… so pure. This book is love and I say it whenever I have a chance. Oh how I love you so much. You cannot even imagine how much I love you. Oh! My daughter I love you so much. Love me first and you will experience the love of man when you first love me. Try this my way and it will be so different when you do things my way and not your way. You will see… you'll see, what I say unto you. Love me first and all these things will be added unto you. Oh! My daughter, love me. Pure love…pure love rains on you. You need it to rain on you. Love floods your heart, mind, and soul.

Love floods you now and you feel my great love and you are free to love. You feel it now and it replaces the pain and captivity right now. It is replaced with my love any mental

Purpose: "Freeing Your Mind"

illness or evil spirits, love replaces. Love is more powerful than them both and love takes over and peace comes to you. You see things so much clearer now. OH! You see clearer! Praise Him! Praise Him! Locks are broken and chains are broken. They are broken and your mind is changed and clearer. I paint the picture now; I paint the picture and clearer things you see. You are free my daughter, oh my daughter you are free.

Love your Daddy

PRAYER
Purpose "Freeing your Mind"

    Lord I pray that my sisters' minds are clear from the clutters of this world. Lord your word states that we are renewed daily. Lord let us be so free to hear your voice in order to follow you. Lord cleanse us and Father purge our hearts so we can walk in our destiny.
    AMEN, so be it.

Purpose: "Freeing Your Mind"

RENEWING
Scriptures

I am sorely afflicted; renew and quicken me (give me life), O Lord, according to Your word! Psalm 119:107

He saved us, not because of any works of righteousness that we had done, but because of His own pity and mercy, by [the] cleansing [bath] of the new birth (regeneration) and renewing of the Holy Spirit, Titus 3:5

Create in me a clean heart, O God, and renew a right, persevering, and steadfast spirit within me. Psalms 51:10

Do not be conformed to this world (this age), [fashioned after and adapted to its external, superficial customs], but be transformed (changed) by the [entire] renewal of your mind [by its new ideals and its new attitude], so that you may prove [for yourselves] what is the good and acceptable and perfect will of God, even the thing which is good and acceptable and perfect [in His sight for you]. Romans 12:2

Therefore we do not become discouraged (utterly spiritless, exhausted, and wearied out through fear). Though our outer man is [progressively] decaying and wasting away, yet our inner self is being [progressively] renewed day after day. 2 Corinthians 4:16

And be constantly renewed in the spirit of your mind [having a fresh mental and spiritual attitude], Ephesians 4:23

But those who wait for the Lord [who expect, look for, and hope in Him] shall change and renew their strength and power; they shall lift their wings and mount up [close to God] as eagles [mount up to the sun]; they shall run and not be weary, they shall walk and not faint or become tired. Isaiah 40:31

And have clothed yourselves with the new [spiritual self], which is [ever in the process of being] renewed and remolded into [fuller and more perfect knowledge upon] knowledge after the image (the likeness) of Him Who created it. Colossians 3:10

CHAPTER 13

Blessings: Honoring God

Though it appears that we only benefit from the blessings from God, there are four others ways blessings operate as well. Blessings and miracles are not only for us. We are blessed to be a blessing to others. Miracles occur to draw the unbelievers. We must not get caught in our material possessions and our own lives in which we think that it is about us. We are to remember that our marriages are a great part of ministry. We are allowed to enjoy our marriages on earth.

Love Letter

Dear Daughter,
True honor comes to me when you recognize that the blessings that I give you are for my kingdom. Blessings are a testament of my goodness. Blessings are the way and the direction that I have you to go, it is for my children. Blessings are for my glory. When I release favor and allow miracles to happen it is for the whole entire body of Christ and for unbelievers. My sweet daughters, I want to pour out my blessings to you. I want to give you that response of the wow factor. I want you to understand that I am your only source. I want you to know that I only take care of what I want to. Be a witness and share the ways of my goodness to the lives

that you touch and come in contact with. Your life is the best testimony your life is the best witness of me. Believe what I say unto you. Believe what I reveal to you. Trust me and see how the blessings honor me.

When you are grateful for the many things that I have done and I continue to give to you, when you practice a charity heart in which you bless others then you have the picture of what I want you to see. When you are in the right position then I can use you to bless others. When others are in need, they will know that the blessing could have only come from me. My children will know that I heard their cries; their intimate and private prayers. They will know that I am real.

Oh! I want you to see the plan of this life! Oh I want you to see how great my kingdom is! Oh I want you to see how you play a great role in my will! Oh! How you need to know that you are my missionaries and my disciples. You are my heirs and you carry on the torch for the victory of your brothers and sisters. It is so important that you walk in love with one another. It is so important that you be that living testimony. It is so important that you be that light. It is so important that your life, lines up with my word.

The world must know of me. They must hear of me from every corner of the earth. They must know of my son, Jesus. They must know that He is the connection that brings them home to me. They must know that the things of this world will pass away and there will be a day of judgment. They must know that I love them so much that the best gift a father could give, was already given, my son. They must know that different versions of the Bible, traditions, dominations, and different faith will all have to confess that Jesus is the true son of me. They must know that everyone will have a chance to know me, love me, and be reconciled with me. They must know that I am a fair and just God. That day will come when I will decide who will be with me for eternity.

Blessings: Honoring God

My daughters hear what I say to you. Life is more than having a husband on earth. Life is more than you having your physical needs met. Life is more than about you.....it is about saving your soul from permanent destruction. Do not miss that. In heaven, it will be no marriages in heaven. There will be no dating in heaven. Heaven will not be how you even think. So why spend your life investing so much energy into temporary matters. Invest your time on heavenly things that will last for eternity. I love you so much and I know that you love me, but you must trust me.

You must put me in the center of your heart. You must make me your only source and I will take care of you better then you could imagine. I pour out so many blessings while you live on earth that others will ask, what is the secret to success? Who is this king that you serve? All things always go back to me. You cannot escape the truth. You cannot eliminate me out of certain areas of your life. I must be the head of them all. Oh my daughters do I love all of you.

You are so beautiful when you line up with my word. The blessings that I have for you will come, one at a time. They will come; I promise you that I will fill your life with so much joy. Oh! Happiness is an understatement of what I have for you but know me first. You must put your trust in only me not a man ... for I am not full of disappointment. Only fulfilled promises come from me. I do not break promises; I do not lie or give false hope. For I am God. If you activate your faith you can have whatever you ask along as it lines up with my word. You can have these things but I must know that I have you. I must know that I can trust you. I must know that I am more than enough in your eyes. I must be convinced that you will cleave to me in the midst of a storm. Then I will hold no good thing......

Hear me because I hear you. Hear me because I know you. Daughter do you know me? Do you recognize my voice? Ask yourself have you spent accurate time with your

Father. Ask yourself do I know this man I call Lord? Do I know my Dad? I love you so much. You are mine and I am yours. Know me, know me and spend time with me because I yearn for the day that you will spend time with me. I am there and will always be. Come and have a real intimate relationship with me. Come and love me, for I love you my dear daughters. Come experience a love that is remarkable. A love that is great. A Love that is terrific. A love that is magnificent. A love that is me, I am God and Sweet dear, I am LOVE.

Love God

Blessings: Honoring God

PRAYER
Blessings Honoring HIM

    Lord I pray that every blessing and gift that you give us, that we will always honor you. Lord I pray that my sisters know that every good and great thing comes from the Father. Let us never forget that you get the glory in our story. Let our hearts stay humble and grateful of your love and generosity. Lord teaches us the way to bless others according to your will. Lord let us remain good stewards over all you give us. Let us use your wisdom when we bless others. Let us yield only to your voice. Lord let us always honor and recognize you in all that we do. Lord let us be your empty vessel in order to be filled up with your purpose and your will.
    AMEN, so be it.

HIS GLORY
Scriptures

I have seen that everything [human] has limits and end [no matter how extensive, noble, and excellent]; but your commandment is exceedingly broad and extends without limits [into eternity] [Rom. 3:10-19.] Psalm 119:96

Then she came and told the man of God. He said, Go, sell the oil and pay your debt, and you and your sons live on the rest. II Kings 4:7

Therefore I [am ready to] persevere and stand my ground with patience and endure everything for the sake of the elect [God's chosen], so that they too may obtain [the] salvation which is in Christ Jesus, with [the reward of] eternal glory. 2 Timothy 2:10

Clothed in God's glory [in all its splendor and radiance]. The luster of it resembled a rare and most precious jewel, like jasper, shining clear as crystal. Revelation 21:11

But he, full of the Holy Spirit and controlled by Him, gazed into heaven and saw the glory (the splendor and majesty) of God, and Jesus standing at God's right hand; Acts 7:55

Through Him also we have [our] access (entrance, introduction) by faith into this grace (state of God's favor) in which we [firmly and safely] stand. And let us rejoice and exult in our hope of experiencing and enjoying the glory of God. Romans 5:2

Blessings: Honoring God

If you are censured and suffer abuse [because you bear] the name of Christ, blessed [are you--happy, fortunate, to be envied, with life-joy, and satisfaction in God's favor and salvation, regardless of your outward condition], because the Spirit of glory, the Spirit of God, is resting upon you. On their part He is blasphemed, but on your part He is glorified. 1 Peter 4:14

And you said, Behold, the Lord our God has shown us His glory and His greatness, and we have heard His voice out of the midst of the fire; we have this day seen that God speaks with man and man still lives. Deuteronomy 5:24

And my God will liberally supply (fill to the full) your every need according to His riches in glory in Christ Jesus. Philippians 4:19

Will You Marry Me?

Blessings: Honoring God

HIS PROMISE

There are so many promises from God. God promises to love, cherish and adore you. His vows and His proposal are very real and true. What are God's Promises?
He has promised never to leave us. He has promised to return to us. He has promised to be whatever we need Him to be. He has promised to love us. There is such a benefit when you seek Him first and desire to want Him more than anything else He promises to give so much than you could not even imagine.
You can only know my promises if you know me. You can only know my promises if you learn me and my Word. How can you know what they are and how to receive them? You must study me and they will be revealed and be at your disposal. Know me, my child and that is what I want you know. My vows to you are so real and my promises are real but they come from studying. The trust and faith that you build up in me comes when you studying my Word and you practice my principles. When you spend little time with me, you only will see little results. When you spend a great deal of time then better days await you. You have to study me. You have to fellowship with me. Then you can have all I promised you. You can have all that I supplied for you. OH! My daughter my promises impact your children and their children. You bless your seed and the seeds to come when you activate your faith....learn me and you will know my promises.....LOVE GOD

HIS LOVE
Scriptures

Nevertheless, the Lord your God would not listen to Balaam, but the Lord your God turned the curse into a blessing to you, because the Lord your God loves you. Deuteronomy 23:5

And therefore the Lord [earnestly] waits [expecting, looking, and longing] to be gracious to you; and therefore He lifts Himself up, that He may have mercy on you and show loving-kindness to you. For the Lord is a God of justice. Blessed (happy, fortunate, to be envied) are all those who [earnestly] wait for Him, who expect and look and long for Him [for His victory, His favor, His love, His peace, His joy, and His matchless, unbroken companionship]! Isaiah 30:18

For God so greatly loved and dearly prized the world that He [even] gave up His only begotten (unique) Son, so that whoever believes in (trusts in, clings to, relies on) Him shall not perish (come to destruction, be lost) but have eternal (everlasting) life. John 3:16

Such hope never disappoints or deludes or shames us, for God's love has been poured out in our hearts through the Holy Spirit Who has been given to us. Romans 5:5

But God shows and clearly proves His [own] love for us by the fact that while we were still sinners, Christ (the Messiah, the Anointed One) died for us. Romans 5:8

Not only so, but we also rejoice and exultingly glory in God [in His love and perfection] through our Lord Jesus

Christ, through whom we have now received and enjoy [our] reconciliation. Romans 5:11

And so faith, hope, love abide [faith--conviction and belief respecting man's relation to God and divine things; hope--joyful and confident expectation of eternal salvation; love--true affection for God and man, growing out of God's love for and in us], these three; but the greatest of these is love. 1 Corinthians 13:13

Finally, brethren, farewell (rejoice)! Be strengthened (perfected, completed, made what you ought to be); be encouraged and consoled and comforted; be of the same [agreeable] mind one with another; live in peace, and [then] the God of love [Who is the Source of affection, goodwill, love, and benevolence toward men] and the Author and Promoter of peace will be with you. 2 Corinthians 13:11

But God--so rich is He in His mercy! Because of and in order to satisfy the great and wonderful and intense love with which He loved us, Ephesians 2:4

Will You Marry Me?

Blessings: Honoring God

THE ANSWER

The question is, *"Will you marry Him?* What is your answer my sisters in Christ? *Will you accept the proposal from your Heavenly Father?* He is a man that will give you everything you ever dreamed and hoped. A man that is strong, wise and honorable that keeps His promises and will never break your heart. A man that knows your thoughts and understand your moods and that can bring you more than happiness but also His unspeakable joy. Jehovah Shalom is a man that will never leave you alone, He is present even when you are physically alone. God will constantly lift you up and never will tear you down.

My answer to the Heavenly Father was, "Yes." Even though my divorce occurred shortly after the marriage, I learned that I had a husband in the Lord. I learned who He was and how to depend on Him. He healed me from all those dark places and made me one of His lights. He taught me that I was beautiful on the inside as well as the outside. All the uncertainties and doubts that plague me for so many years about who I was, God corrected my wrong thinking. He healed me of those deep pains and severe hurts that haunted me for many years. The greatest deliverance my Savior did for me was brought me out of depression which no man had the power to do. For the deliverance that He gave me, it is impossible for me to forget. The experiences that I went through did not tear me down but motivated me to walk in my destiny. God had a purpose for my life and though many trials and mistakes occurred in my past, He used them for His glory. Wow!

Therefore, ladies will you take the vow to marry such a man? Will you say I do? Will you be excited about a lifetime and eternity with HIM? Will you be excited about learning HIM? Are you willing to fall in love with HIM… a man that is guaranteed to give you the first date of a lifetime?

Yes, He has invited you on a date. A date so wonderful you will keep wanting more and more. The closer you come to this man the more you want to know Him. The more time you spend, the more you crave Him. Then He truly becomes your new hidden desire. He becomes your friend your ultimate soul mate. Before you say I do or I will, you must know HIM. The best decision that you could make, is saying yes to a date with Jesus. Let HIM wine and dine you and romance you and lastly let HIM love on you. A true commitment that is true and very much real.

This Book of the Law shall not depart out of your mouth, but you shall meditate on it day and night, that you may observe and do according to all that is written in it. For then you shall make your way prosperous, and then you shall deal wisely and have good success. ***Joshua 1:8***

Blessings: Honoring God

YOUR LOVE FOR HIM
Scriptures

We are assured and know that [God being a partner in their labor] all things work together and are [fitting into a plan] for good to and for those who love God and are called according to [His] design and purpose. Romans 8:28

And He replied to him, You shall love the Lord your God with all your heart and with all your soul and with all your mind (intellect). Matthew 22:37

Nor height nor depth, nor anything else in all creation will be able to separate us from the love of God which is in Christ Jesus our Lord. Romans 8:39

But if one loves God truly [with affectionate reverence, prompt obedience, and grateful recognition of His blessing], he is known by God [recognized as worthy of His intimacy and love, and he is owned by Him]. I Corinthians 8:3

You [are like] unfaithful wives [having illicit love affairs with the world and breaking your marriage vow to God]! Do you not know that being the world's friend is being God's enemy? So whoever chooses to be a friend of the world takes his stand as an enemy of God. James 4:4

For the [true] love of God is this: that we do His commands [keep His ordinances and are mindful of His precepts and teaching]. And these orders of His are not irksome (burdensome, oppressive, or grievous). I John 5:3

And may love the Lord your God, obey His voice, and cling to Him. For He is your life and the length of your days, that you may dwell in the land which the Lord swore to give to your fathers, to Abraham, Isaac, and Jacob. Deuteronomy 30:20

But take diligent heed to do the commandment and the law which Moses the servant of the Lord charged you: to love the Lord your God and to walk in all His ways and to keep His commandments and to cling to and unite with Him and to serve Him with all your heart and soul [your very life]. Joshua 22:5

THEREFORE BE imitators of God [copy Him and follow His example], as well-beloved children [imitate their father]. And walk in love, [esteeming and delighting in one another] as Christ loved us and gave Himself up for us , a slain offering and sacrifice to God for you, so that it became a sweet fragrance. [Ezek. 20:41.] Ephesians 5:1-2

Blessings: Honoring God

PERSONAL REFLECTIONS

Will You Marry Me?

Blessings: Honoring God

Will You Marry Me?

ABOUT THE AUTHOR

Chiffone Nicole is a native of Detroit, Michigan. She currently resides in Memphis, Tennessee with her intelligent and gifted son, JohnDavid. Not only is she a devoted mother, she is dedicated to the community as social worker. She has worked for nearly fifteen years helping children, youth, and families. For over seven years she has worked in school districts across the country in which she has impacted hundreds by providing resources, guidance, and counseling.

Her love for God and faith has been the driving force behind her ministry. At an early age of 12 she accepted Christ and had a heart for God's people. During this time she experienced signs and wonders from God. She knew in high school that she had a passion for serving others and that she was motivated to help and did so in numerous volunteer experiences. Though she faced many obstacles when applying for school, she prevailed because of her Faith in God and herself. Not only did she complete her Bachelor degree in spite of her father passing in her last year of school, she earned a 3.4 GPA in the Social Work program.

Determine to excel in her profession she furthered her education by obtaining a Master Degree in Social Work from Wayne State University. Not only did she develop academically over the years she went on to develop spiritually by studying the Word and enrolling in ministry school.

Her true passion is for ministering to God's People through prayer. She has a unique calling on her life in which she taps into the spiritual ram through constant prayer and fasting. She truly believes that Prayer and Fasting are both a sure connection to hear from God. She is involved in the Prayer Ministry in which she has been an effective intercessory prayer. She is also a faithful minister for the Children's Church.

Chiffone Nicole is a proud and an active member of Alpha Kappa Alpha Sorority Inc, an organization dedicated to sisterhood and service. With this connection she has been able to work with like-minded women who believe in uplifting the community and serving all mankind.

For the past several years she has watched God develop and transform her and she is extremely excited about the transformation that is taking take place in your life. She is confident that the Word of God works but knows that you must work the Word by activating your faith, speaking, and practicing God's principles. She was instructed to write the book, *"Will You Marry Me?"* She was obedient to the voice of the Lord and hopes that women will be healed and delivered from their past hurts and pains by seeking the Heavenly Father to make them whole. Her ultimate desire is to encourage women across the world to walk in their destiny. The Statement that she lives by is, "To God Be the Glory."